1,001 Tips on Practicing, Perfecting and Performing Your Act

For jugglers and other variety Artists

—⁌———————(•)———————⁌—

Collected and compiled

By

Daniel Holzman

1,001 Tips on Practicing, Perfecting and Performing Your Act

For Jugglers and Other Variety Artists

Collected and compiled
By Daniel Holzman

ISBN: 198513554X

Cover photos: Front Left to right: Robert Nelson,
Daniel Holzman, Barry Friedman (Raspyni Brothers),
Bri Crabtree, Cliff Spenger, Jack Kalvan,
Rick Rubenstein (Clockwork), Kevin Axtell.
Back Left to Right: David Cain, Owen Morse, John Wee
(The Passing Zone), Niels Duinker, Glenn Singer, David
Aiken, Johnny Fox, Steve Langley, Karen Quest.

Disclaimer

The information in this book is meant to supplement, not replace, proper juggling and stunt training. Any performance involving equipment, balance and environmental factors, (juggling and performance stunts) poses some inherent risk. The author and publisher advise readers to take full responsibility for their safety and know their limits. Before practicing the skills described in this book, be sure that your equipment is well maintained, and do not take risks beyond your level of experience, aptitude, training, and comfort level.

Acknowledgements

I would like to thank the entire variety arts community, especially the following performers and friends for their help in contributing to the tips found in this book:

David Aiken, Fred Anderson, Kevin Axtell, Barry Bakalor, Matt Baker, Mitchel Barrett, Howie & Bert, Aaron Bonk, Randy Brake, Jason Byrne, David Cain, Eden Cheung, Michael Chrrick, Bri Crabtree, Sean and Dave, Ben Decker, Greg DeSanto, Niels Duinker, Arsene Dupin, Jack Erickson, Johnny Fox, Dick Franco, Barry Friedman, Greg Frisbee, Jay Gilligan, Toto Johnson, The Boogie-Down Jugglers, Jack Kalvan, Steve Langley, Barry Lubin, Jim Mackenzie, Kirk Marsh, Casey Martin, Scotty Meltzer, Bob Mendelsohn, Dan Menendez, Owen Morse, Robert Nelson, Mark Nizer, John Park, Charlie Peachock, Karen Quest, Jim Ridgley Rick Rubenstein, Glenn Singer, Cliff Spenger, Wacky Chad, David Walbridge, Thom Wall, John Wee, Rob Williams, Evan Young, & Alex Zerbe

Special thanks to my wife Karen Holzman for her design and layout of this book.

Table of Contents

Introduction

Books on show business have played a very important role in my development as an entertainer. I first learned to juggle in 1974 by reading "The Juggling Book" by Carlo, and it was Karl Heinz Ziethen's book "4000 Years of Juggling" that inspired me to become a full-time performer. Going from being someone who "juggles" to becoming a professional "juggler" was a big step and I wish that I had a book like "1,001 Tips on Practicing, Perfecting and Performing Your Act" to help me make that transition.

I think it's better to learn how important it is to shake excess fuel off torches before juggling them from a book rather than from hot gas flying in to your eyes during your first street show, and I definitely would have preferred learning how slippery brand new silicon balls are by reading about it sitting at home on my couch, rather than during an international juggling competition.

I've learned a lot from the mistakes I've made during my 35 years as a variety performer. The advice collected in this book is your chance to learn this stuff in an easier way. So, DON'T BLOW IT! I'm sure that if you take advantage of this opportunity, your future Book of Tips will start with this one:

#1 Buy "1001 Tips on Practicing, Perfecting and Performing Your Act" the first chance you get.

Foreword
-- By Niels Duinker

I met Daniel Holzman for the first time in Las Vegas in 2004 and then again at the I.J.A. Convention in 2006. A few weeks after our second meeting he graciously invited me to his home near San Francisco where he worked with me on my act for several days. Over the years we have become really good friends and the fact that my life as a professional juggler continues to treat me extremely well is in no small part due to Daniel's mentoring.

From Skype calls to live coaching sessions, Daniel has helped me enormously with the both the development of my show and the planning of my career. For most of my juggling career Daniel's first book was out of print and unknown to me, but I was lucky enough to have had Daniel there in real life giving me loads of tips first hand. And although I made my share of mistakes when I started out Daniel's advice has helped me avoid making many more.

The hours of work that have been put into my juggling show over the years have paid off for me enormously and I'm proud to say that as a juggler, I have performed on all 7 continents, appeared on numerous television shows all over the world, won many prestigious and coveted awards, and been granted a special performance visa for the United States.

Daniel's Tip #821 has definitely become a reality for me: Juggling is a real job!

I'd like to thank Daniel for putting out the new version of his tip book, and I hope that the reader will take full advantage of this great information!

Niels Duinker, Professional Juggler from the Netherlands. www.comedyjuggler.com

Forword
-- by Barry Friedman

In July of 1982, Dan Holzman and I climbed into my brand new car and started driving. Our goal was to get to the Chicago Renaissance Festival and do a few shows. We had no name, no act, no costumes, and very few props. Our inventory of belongings: gas money, a few snacks, and desire.

One thing led to another and before you could say "Johnny Carson," The Raspyni Brothers were being invited back for a second appearance on *The Tonight Show*.

"WAIT A SECOND, BARRY!!! Surely you are skipping over some of the details."

Of course I am – those were some tough lessons we learned. Just because Dan wants to give away 35 years worth of "street smarts" for a lousy 15 bucks, doesn't mean I have to.

No way – not gonna do it. Go ahead, practice with sharp knives. By all means, treat your audience like a bad crowd when they aren't laughing at your jokes. Oh yeah, and as for silicon balls getting slippery when they are new – don't worry, your hands probably won't sweat.

It is always good to read an author who writes about what he knows – at least Dan isn't writing a book about computers!

But now let me get past all this tomfoolery and artificial anger. You're motivated to improve and that's why you bought this book – good for you! My job is to discourage any sense of buyer's remorse you might be feeling and to tell you some good things about the author. This will be easy.

The guy is a comedy wizard, a human CD-ROM on juggling and performing. He is also highly motivated and always willing to share his knowledge with anyone who will listen (and now, with anyone who can read).

What I gained most from this book is the reminder that learning is a life-long process. I have watched Dan learn most of these lessons and have also seen him work very hard at putting together this manuscript. Absorb what you read - it will make that life-long process of learning a much smoother road.

Oh yeah – and one more tip that isn't in the book: You know that voice Dan uses on stage? It only works for him.

Barry Friedman, The Taller Raspyni Brother www.raspyni.com

Fire Juggling

1. Choices for fuel: White gas/camping fuel (lights quickly with not much smoke). Charcoal lighter (easy to get and burns for a long time). Lamp oil (smells nicer, has a long burn time, but is harder to light). Paraffin (the least toxic choice if fire eating is also on the menu).

2. Some jugglers will use a mixture of fuel such as lamp oil for a longer burn with a squirt of charcoal lighter so it catches faster.

3. One top professional recommends four parts white gas to one part lamp oil.

4. BBQ starter fluid is safer than white gas because of the high flash point. It is almost impossible to light accidentally.

5. I personally use Coleman brand camping fuel.

6. Not recommend: automobile gasoline, very smoky and unhealthy to breath, and can hurt if it comes in contact with your skin.

7. Buy professional juggling torches. The danger of homemade torches breaking or coming apart is not worth any money you might save.

8. Inspect your fire props closely before you go out to use them in a show.

9. Store fuel in a tightly sealed metal container. A plastic container will degrade over time.

10. Over the life of the fire prop, lighter fluid will degrade the kevlar wicks and cause them to burn a shorter period of time.

11. Ammo cans are a good choice for storing fuel, and can be found at military supply stores.

12. A funnel can be a useful tool if pouring fuel into a dipping cup or can.

13. I find it more convenient if the mouth of the fuel container is large enough for dipping the torches, because that way I don't need to pour the fuel into a separate metal cup before I dip them.

14. Glass jars are fine for making Molotov cocktails, not for dipping torches. A glass fuel container is strongly not recommended.

15. Keep torch fuel a safe distance away from where you'll be juggling. (MINIMUM 20 FEET).

16. Make sure you have a fire extinguisher handy.

17. A good all-purpose fire extinguisher is one designated ABC.

18. Make sure it is full by checking the indicator on the extinguisher (should be in the green) and check the pressure gauge.

19. A good acronym to remember when using a fire extinguisher is P.A.S.S. (Pull the Pin, Aim the nozzle at the base of the fire, Squeeze the lever slowly, Sweep side to side).

20. Be careful when wearing loose flowing clothing. The lighter the fabric and the looser the weave the faster it will catch fire.

21. Make sure your sleeves are not too long and will not get hung up on the handles of the torches.

22. Never perform fire juggling while wearing heavy hairspray.

23. If you catch on fire always remember: Stop, Drop, Cover your face and Roll.

24. It is a good idea to have a person designated off stage as a safety to prevent fire related accidents.

25. Learn the classes of burns and how to care for them.

26. For minor burns where the skin is intact and not peeling, immerse the burn in cold water for five minutes, and when the skin is cooled and dry, apply antibiotic ointment or cream.

27. If small blisters form, it is recommended to not pop them.

28. A good burn relief spray will contain Aloe and Lidocaine and it is recommended to keep one in your prop bag.

29. Remember the above tips are not formal medical instructions. Always consult a doctor for proper medical treatment if necessary.

30. Make sure the client that you will be performing for knows that you'll be using fire and has obtained the proper permits.

31. Before lighting the torches, shake excess fuel off them in a safe area away from the audience and anything flammable, that way excess gas won't fly in your eyes when you are juggling.

32. If you dip your torches before the show starts, and have to wait before using them, keep them in an airtight tube or wrap them in a plastic bag to keep the fuel from evaporating.

33. Practice lit torch juggling or any other type of fire performance in the dark before you do for the first time in front of an audience. Fire juggling is much different and more difficult in the dark.

34. To keep the flames from blowing in your face, if possible turn your back to the wind or stand sideways to the wind when juggling torches outdoors.

35. When doing street show, there is no law that says you can't bring your own lighter (it is an overused and standard gag to borrow one from a member of the audience).

36. When juggling torches or any other fire props, try to stay at least ten feet away from anything flammable (including audience members).

37. Be insured (for information on the World Clown Association group coverage contact them at: (800)-336-7922.

38. When performing fire indoors (after getting permission and proper permits of course), make sure the smoke won't set off any fire alarms, leave a black mark on the ceiling, or make it difficult for the audience to breathe.

39. Juggling smoking black sticks isn't very impressive. Plan out your fire routine so that the torches remain lit until your last trick is over.

40. Audiences are glad to scream out the obvious, in an obnoxious fashion when a torch goes out.

41. A couple of alternatives to blowing out torches are to extinguish them in an airtight box, or smother them with a fireproof blanket. (Duvetyne fireproof fabric is an excellent fire suppression tool).

42. Fire extinguishers are notoriously messy and can ruin equipment and costumes when used.

43. Wipe off torch handles before re-using them again to keep them clean, and if doing shows back to back prevent any gas or soot from making them slippery.

44. After dipping the torches don't immediately turn them right side up (with the handles pointing down), because fuel can drip on the handles and cause them to get slippery.

45. Never re-dip a torch that was just used (even if it seems like it is completely out). This is an extremely important safety tip!

46. Used torch wicks are dirty, wrap them up (make sure they are cool first), in plastic, a cloth bag or a towel before placing them in your prop case.

47. To keep the rest of your equipment clean, consider having a separate prop bag for your fire props.

48. Be careful if any gas drips from the torches and makes the floor slippery for your later routines or any act that has to follow you on stage.

49. If a dirty torch wick touches your silicon balls you could end up with them being permanently stained from the resulting black marks.

50. To keep from getting black sooty spots on your costume before the show, do not wear it while warming up with used unlit torches.

51. Worn down torch wicks will not burn as long as new ones, and tend to drip fuel when juggled.

52. Old torches have been known to break in mid-air. Replace them before this happens. A blazing torch wick flying into your audience can add excitement to your show, but it is not recommended.

53. When in doubt, throw it out. Err on the side of caution.

54. When traveling by air make sure all the fuel is burned off your torch wicks (The vapor can accumulate if you don't), air them out, and wrap them in plastic to prevent any smell of gasoline.

55.   Invest in a good butane windproof lighter for lighting fire props outside in the wind.

56.   Light colored handles (instead of black ones) are much easier to see in dark conditions.

57.   In high winds, experiment with a tighter faster pattern that is juggled further away from your body than usual, and avoid high throws that can be blown off course.

58.   For less smoke indoors, try Coleman fuel mixed with isopropyl alcohol.

59.   If you can't find regular fuel, try fingernail polish remover it works well in a pinch and has a nice smell.

Fire Eating and Blowing

60.   Caution: Fire eating and fire blowing are two of the most dangerous variety skills you can learn. I suggest learning these two skills with safety as your first priority.

61.   If at all possible, learn from an expert entertainer who has a lot of real world experience in these performance skills.

62.   Always practice and perform these skills with proper fire safety tools on hand (see tips under fire juggling).

63.   Fire eating is easier than fire blowing and of the two, I recommend you learn this first.

64. The mouth is coated with a layer of saliva. This allows the fire eater to extinguish a small torch by placing it in their mouth and smothering the flame.

65. Fire eating torches are usually much smaller than fire juggling torches.

66. A juggling torch can be used if the performer's mouth is big enough, but because of the larger flame, it is not recommended for beginners.

67. Fire eating fuel is known as Kerosene in the U.S. and as is also known as Paraffin or lamp oil.

68. Make sure your fuel is not scented nor has any other harmful additives.

69. Fire eating torches are usually made of aluminum, avoid any metal (such as steel) that will heat up and cause burns to your lips or mouth.

70. After dipping and lighting the torch, tilt your head back so your mouth points straight upwards.

71. Make sure to touch no other part of your face with the flame as you lower it into your mouth.

72. Don't inhale! Blow out as you lower the torch keeping the flame off your lips.

73. Close your mouth around the torch starving it of oxygen and extinguishing it.

74. Understand that every time you do fire eating you are ingesting some of the fuel through the lining of your mouth. My suggestion is you limit the num-

ber of times you perform this stunt, and seriously consider if the entertainment value is worth the possible ill effects on your health.

75. The heat of the torch, especially if the torch is allowed to burn in the mouth for any length of time can also damage your teeth, proceed with caution!

76. When doing this stunt more than once, make sure no excess gas has gotten on your chin or around your mouth. This could lead to serious burns if ignited.

77. Fire Blowing should only be learned under the personal instruction of a skilled instructor who has had years of experience in the art.

78. Dangers include swallowing toxic additives in the fuel, getting fuel in the lungs, and in extreme cases, the fuel can actually ignite inside your body. Proceed with great caution.

79. Start by learning to spray water from your mouth in a powerful mist with the full force of the lungs.

80. The water should come out in a fine spray from a narrow gap between the lips.

81. At the end of the blast of water, the mouth should be immediately clamped tightly shut. It is very important not to inhale for several moments. This is to insure that when working with actual fuel it doesn't get drawn back into the lungs.

82.   When you feel you have mastered this skill with water, it is time to try it with actual fuel. It takes a while to get used to the taste and you must be able to hold it in your mouth without gagging.

83.   To ignite the sprayed fuel, use a fire eating or juggling torch.

84.   Start with a small gulp of fuel, and use a forceful blast from your mouth to ignite the aerated fuel spray using the flame of the torch.

85.   Once the spray is ignited, quickly remove the torch from in front of your mouth. The fuel will continue to burn as it is sprayed out of your mouth.

86.   The stream of fuel is cut off by closing the mouth in mid blow, the head is turned away, and the resulting fire ball will launch into the air and die away.

87.   Once again it is strongly urged that extreme caution is taken when learning and performing fire blowing.

88.   If repeating this stunt make sure all excess fuel is wiped from the mouth and chin.

89.   It is also strongly advised to try alternatives to using actual fuel. Corn starch and Cocoa powder are two such options that can be blown in a fine mist from the mouth and be ignited.

90.   Always make sure to have a plan for and the safety equipment necessary for emergencies.

91.   Never perform this stunt alone, and always take into consideration your personal safety, and the safety of the audiences you perform for.

Sword Swallowing

92.   It is too dangerous to attempt to learn sword swallowing from a book. If you wish to learn this variety art form, you will need to find an experienced performer willing to teach you in person.

93.   Possible side effects and dangers of sword swallowing include: Throat pain, injury to the esophagus, internal bleeding, esophageal perforations, Pleurisy (inflammation of the lungs), Pericarditis (inflammation of the sac that covers the heart). ❖

Knife Juggling

94.   A juggling knife doesn't have to be sharp to look sharp.

95.   Perceived danger by the audience is always preferable in a show to real danger to the performer.

96.   Before using another juggler's knives, make sure they are aware of tip #94.

97.   Cutting a carrot on stage is a common way of verifying a knife's sharpness. (It is always recommended that you be an original performer and that you come up with alternatives to anything that is done in the common way).

98.   Prepare a home-made machete knife blade for juggling by dulling it on a grinder, rounding off the point, and getting it chromed.

99.   I recommend buying professional juggling knives from a reputable prop maker. (A good one for custom knives is Three Finger Juggling).

100.   A dropped knife can easily mar a stage floor or damage a microphone cord, so be safe, be aware of your surroundings and put down a mat when possible.

101.   Be especially careful juggling over a floor made of tile, or any other breakable material that could crack if a knife is dropped on it.

102. When not in use, keep knives sheathed separately to keep them from being scratched or chipped.

103. Keep unsheathed knives away from silicon balls or other props because they can cut gashes into them if stored together.

104. Even though the knives you will be using are dull, treat them as if they were sharp to maintain the illusion of danger. Don't handle them by the blade or toss them around in a casual manner.

105. When passing knives make sure there is enough room behind you for a missed knife to land safely.

106. If you plan to pass knives around a volunteer, make sure they know exactly what they are getting into, give them detailed understandable directions, and make sure they are not impaired by drugs or drink in any way.

107. If you do a knife pass around a volunteer, check to make sure this type of stunt will be covered by your insurance policy.

108. Dropping your knives on pavement can scratch them, chip them and cause them to have dangerous sharp spots on the edge of the blade.

109. A knife blade can get rusty if left in the rain and put away wet.

110. If you are going to juggle sickles, consider juggling them with the points facing up. This gives them an elegant look, and helps to make them appear more dangerous to the audience (I personally juggle them point down).

111. Make sure when juggling knives outdoors, that you are not blinded by the sun flashing off the blades. ❖

Unicycling

112.   When learning to ride a unicycle, wear appropriate clothing and safety equipment. Knee, elbow, wrist pads, and helmet are recommended.

113.   Shorts with pads built in are common for other sports and can be used to protect your tailbone in case of a fall.

114.   Watch out for dangling shoelaces, and make sure your shoes are appropriate for riding a unicycle (no flip flops).

115.   If you're having trouble learning to ride a small unicycle, try using ski poles to help you balance.

116.   A narrow hallway where you can touch both side walls is a great place to learn.

117.   Attempting to mount a giraffe unicycle while wearing pants that are loose in the crotch (i.e. sweatpants), can cause serious injury.

118.   Learn to free mount a giraffe unicycle on hard packed grass. (A fall is less likely to result in injury).

119.   Try to learn with other people around, so in case of emergency help can be at hand.

120.   Sit up and look straight ahead, not down.

121.   Lean forward to go forward.

122.　Make sure the spokes and chain (on a giraffe) are adequately tightened.

123.　Adjust the seat so your leg is extended when the pedal is down, but leave a slight bend in the knee.

124.　You don't want to be on your tip toes on the pedals.

125.　Put most of your body weight on the seat, and not on the pedals.

126.　Toe-clips that keep your foot fastened to the pedal can be used when hopping or jumping rope, but be careful of the additional danger.

127.　A small block placed behind the unicycle tire will keep it from rolling backwards, and make the unicycle easier to mount.

128.　Before riding a six-foot unicycle, make sure there's enough room to safely dismount.

129.　If you plan to ride a 22-foot unicycle in your street show, make sure you weigh the risk versus the reward.

130.　If you have a volunteer or someone who isn't a unicycle rider themselves help you mount a giraffe unicycle, make sure they know to keep their fingers away from the chain.

131.　If you find yourself peddling back and forth in a quick and jerky manner, it probably means you are putting too much of your weight on the pedals.

132. From an audience's point of view a unicycle with an under-inflated tire looks easier to ride.

133. On uneven surfaces like cobblestone, deflate the tire a little more to make idling easier.

134. When traveling to a show, bring a tire pump and a spare inner-tube.

135. A padded seat may come in handy when learning to jump rope or ride down stairs on your unicycle.

136. When attempting to jump rope on a unicycle, use your thighs to grip the seat and try placing your feet on the cranks not the pedals.

137. If you have a volunteer throw you a prop while up on a giraffe, be careful that it doesn't land on the ground near the unicycle's tire because this could cause you to fall.

138. If you are free mounting a tall unicycle where you can't comfortably reach the first pedal with your less favored foot, start with that foot on top of the tire.

139. Use that foot as a brake by wedging against the frame. Place your other foot on the pedal and mount the unicycle from that position.

140. A giraffe unicycle is usually 5 feet tall or more, to an audience it seems more difficult to balance on than a small unicycle, but the height actually makes it easier.

141. Don't be surprised when you first are riding a giraffe that you seem higher in the air than you really are. It is scary at first, but you can get comfortable with enough practice.

142. Learning to juggle while you idle (rocking back and forth in one place), is easier than you might think. Many jugglers find it less difficult to juggle on a tall unicycle compared to a standard size one. ❖

Rola-Bola

143. If you are looking to add a balancing skill to your act, the Rola-Bola can be an option. I find it easier than the unicycle for beginners to learn.

144. A rubber mat placed under the roller (the tube that is placed under the Rola-Bola board) can help prevent it from sliding out from under you as you balance on the board.

145. It also helps when performing on the street or other uneven surfaces to bring a mat or board to place the roller on.

146. Small wooden blocks can be attached under the ends of the board. This helps to keep the board in one place, and prevents it from sliding out from under you when you do a basic Rola-Bola mount.

147. Most performers will perform the Rola-Bola with it up on a small table or prop case. This doesn't add much difficulty, but it does add to the danger and entertainment factor. Also, when you are working on the street, it makes it much easier to see, and gives you a consistent surface to balance on.

148. Performing the Rola-Bola on a small stand or stool can be very dangerous. When considering the safety of the stunt, make sure there is enough room for the roller to move from side to side under the balance board.

149.   Another way to add height to a Rola-Bola stunt is to use two balance boards with wooden blocks (cigar boxes work well) placed between them.

150.   You can replace the wooden blocks with other sturdy objects such as bottles or heavy drinking glasses to add even another level of entertainment value.

151.   The roller can also be replaced with a sturdy ball (bowling ball) to add a different look and make the Rola-Bola a bit more of a precarious stunt.

152.   Many skilled Rola-Bola performers will add multiple levels to the Rola-Bola with additional rollers and metal spacers, or perform stunts on the Rola-Bola like jumping rope or juggling.

153.   Acrobatic stunts such as handstands or two-man high can also be performed on the Rola-Bola. ❖

Free Standing Ladder

154. A free standing ladder is a custom made ladder that can be balanced on, in a similar manner as you would use for a pair of peg stilts.

155. It is wider then a regular ladder, at least 6 feet tall with all the rungs evenly spaced except the top rung which is a bit farther apart than the others.

156. The free standing ladder is also referred to as the balancing ladder or walking ladder.

157. When learning the ladder, a hallway where you can turn the ladder sideways and have enough room to practice but won't be able to fall forward or backward can be useful.

158. The floor should be level and smooth, if on grass make sure it is hard packed and the legs of the ladder won't sink in to it.

159. Most falls from the ladder will be forward or backwards, not to one side or the other.

160. When learning, a spotter (someone to help you maintain the balance or prevent you from falling) is recommended.

161. Start with the ladder at a slight angle away from your body; pull it towards you as you mount the first rung.

162. Your hands are on the sides of the ladder near or on the top of it at an equal height opposite each other.

163. Bring your hips in close to the ladder, don't arch your body away from it.

164. You balance and stabilize yourself on the ladder by rocking side to side (never front to back).

165. This side to side motion is also referred to as waddling.

166. As you climb the rungs of the ladder each foot moves up while the weight is on the other foot. The legs of the ladder lift off the ground momentarily as the ladder shifts from side to side.

167. You want to drive the upward motion with your legs not your arms. Keep enough pressure with your hands and arms to keep the ladder steady.

168. If you rely on your arms too much it will be difficult to learn to let go and balance without them.

169. Don't be surprised at the steep learning curve, it might seem as if you are making no progress at first, but keep at it and it will become doable.

170. Make sure you are very comfortable balancing on the lower rung before attempting the climb higher. You will find it is easier to start learning the balance on the 2nd or 3rd then on the 1st rung since the center of balance is a little higher.

171. On most balancing ladders, both the side rails of the ladder and the rungs are round and not rectangular.

172. Having the rungs closer together (about 8") allows you to take smaller steps as you climb and looks smoother.

173. Some expert ladder balancers use foot pedestals on the very top to stand on. (This is very advanced and should only be attempted with expert supervision).

174. Keep the rocking motion going at all times while you are climbing and balancing on the ladder.

175. Keep your feet pressed against the inside sides of the ladder for greater stability.

176. When you get to the 4th rung, move your hands to the top of the ladder side rails.

177. The step over of the top rail with one leg is considered to be the most perilous move of the balance. Make sure you are extremely solid on the lower rungs before you attempt it.

178. You can perform the step over with both hands on the ladder or by quickly removing and then re-gripping with one of your hands as you swing over your leg.

179. Always make sure the fall radius around you is clear.

180. If you feel as if you are losing your balance, it is always better to try to jump off under control than fall off.

181. Make sure your knees and ankles are strong and can handle the stress of jumping off the ladder. Most of the time your weight will come down on just one foot or the other as you jump.

182. Stepping over the top rung and having one leg on each side of the ladder is what allows you to have your hands free to perform juggling or other stunts.

183. Lean a slight bit forward when you step over (usually with your favored leg). Do not lean backwards.

184. When you let go with your hands, you must press your legs tightly against the rungs and take immediate control with your legs.

185. You grip the ladder tightly with your knees or thighs. You want to find a fleshy part of your leg for the rung to press against.

186. Knees pads can be used to make this more comfortable since the pressure against your legs can be painful, especially if you find the rung presses against your shin bone when you grip the ladder.

187. Do not attempt the step over of the top rung wearing baggy pants as they can be caught on the top of the side rails of the ladder.

188. If you want to learn to juggle while balanced on the ladder, have someone ready to hand you or throw you the props. It is very difficult to climb the ladder with props in your hands.

189. When learning the juggle on the ladder, keep your eyes gazing forward towards a distant spot. Keep your head up and don't look down.

190. Do not try to dismount with the juggling props still in your hands.

191. To dismount perform a reverse of the step over, get both legs on the same side of the ladder, then climb or slide down.

192. The climb down is a little different than the climb up and a valuable skill to learn. If you hop off the ladder every time, the impact will add up and cause you physical problems with your knees and ankles over time. ❖

Stilts

193. Peg stilts are more difficult to balance on for long periods of time compared to construction style stilts since you have to keep in constant movement to maintain the balance.

194. When on stilts, it is very difficult to see low obstacles like wires, curbs, tree roots, etc., so keen awareness of your surroundings is always vital.

195. People will want to take pictures with you when you are on stilts, but be careful they don't lean on you or put their arms around your legs in a forceful manner.

196. Keep your stills in good condition; be especially aware of the straps that fasten around your legs. If one were to break or come loose, you have nothing else to connect you to the stilt.

197. Keep focused and alert while getting dressed and set up on the stilts backstage, as this can be one of the most dangerous parts of the procedure. ❖

Blockhead

198. The nail up the nose trick is also known as "The Human Blockhead.

199. The stunt is first learned with a shorter and thinner object without a point.

200. A cue tip is a good first choice.

201. Make sure to wet the cue tip shaft (saliva is fine), so it is a bit slippery, and won't scrape if the nasal passage is dry.

202. One key point to realize is, that cue tip goes not go up the nose, but straight back (parallel to the ground) into the nasal cavity also called the Nasopharynx.

203. It helps if the nasal passageway is clear, a Neti pot (uses water to clean out the nose) can be a good tool to use before trying the blockhead, and will also help if you suffer from nasal infections.

204. You will find that one side of your nose will be more open and the passage way will be straighter and easier to use. This is different for each person, but the left side seems more common.

205. When pushing the cue tip straight into your nose back, understand that you should never have to force it. There will be a little bit of resistance as it goes under a flap of skin, but it should take no real effort.

206. Make sure to leave some of the cue tip outside your nose. The passageway is long enough to get the whole thing inside your nose but you want to be able to grab the end and easily pull it back out.

207. After getting comfortable with the cue tip, other objects leading up to trying a nail can be a bit longer and wider like plastic stir sticks or the temple pieces of a pair of eyeglasses.

208. When choosing a nail, you might have good luck at a smaller mom-and-pop style hardware store that sells nails by the pound. The size that is most commonly used is a 40 penny nail.

209. A 20 penny nail is good to start with and a 60 penny nail is doable but is thicker and will be more difficult to fit up the nasal canal.

210. File the end of the nail to make it smoother, and make sure there are no barbs on the shaft that could be irritating. A metal file can be used for this purpose.

211. The nail can be driven about 3 ½ to 4 inches up the nose, you will feel a natural stopping place as the nail hits the top of the throat. Never force it past this point.

212. With a longer nail about ¼ to ½ will remain sticking out. If you perform this trick you will have to decide if it is better if the entire nail up to the head goes in or if you feel the audience likes to see more of the nail remain sticking out.

213. Most performers will use a hammer or another hard object like a glass bottle to tap the nail up the nose. It is important to note that you will be using the fingers of the other hand to hold the nail in place so that you can control the amount of force that actually is driving the nail into your nose.

214. If you are performing this trick over and over in a dry environment it is possible to irritate the capillaries in the nose, and a small nose bleed could occur.

215. Other objects that are used for this stunt are screwdrivers and even electric drills. Of course as a performer, you are always encouraged to come up with your own original variations.

216. If you plan on having a volunteer remove the nail, make sure they are sober and intelligent enough to know the danger of behaving in a reckless manner.

217. Great care should be taken that they don't bump the nail, or cause you in any way to lose your balance. I have never heard of a performer falling face first with a nail sticking up their nose, but as you can imagine that would be a very bad scenario.

218. A slight inhale as the volunteer removes the nail can give more resistance and add to the illusion that the nail is firmly lodged in the nose.

219. Washing off the nail after you are done and keeping it in a clean sterile place between shows is recommended. ❖

Clowning

220. Your make-up is your identity, take the time to do it right.

221. Give yourself a longer time as you get older to get ready. Good make-up requires clear vision and a steady hand.

222. Research how your make-up can be copyrighted.

223. It is a cardinal sin to copy another clown's make-up.

224. Try different brands of professional clown make-up to identify the best type for your skin.

225. End by using a coating of powder to keep the make-up from sweating off.

226. Always carry your own hand mirror, and a small make-up repair kit.

227. Get a professional quality wig, wearing one can get quite hot, so consider options when working outside in the heat.

228. Make sure to get your costume professionally cleaned between engagements.

229. The biggest call for clowns is "Home town clowning" working at local events like birthday parties. There is not as much call for circus and theater clowns as in the past.

230. There is a greater call for female clowns. By average most clowns are women in their 40's.

231. As a party clown the key is to have fun and take the audience with you.

232. Remember "If you're not enjoying it, neither will they."

233. Get used to wearing the nose, it takes a while not to notice it in your field of vision.

234. For make-up, keep your palate clean and use good brushes.

235. The big clown shoes also take some getting used to, so practice while wearing them.

236. You need more than just the make-up and costume, it's clowning not a beauty competition.

237. Know when to turn it off! It's tough to be around someone who is "on" 24-hours-a-day.

238. Don't leave the funny backstage.

239. On longer gigs, always remember to pace yourself. This is especially important when working multi-day contracts without a break.

240. Store your rubber nose inside a cut open tennis ball to keep it in shape. ❖

Bubbleology

241. Performing with soap bubbles is also called bubble artistry or Bubbleology.

242. 2 popular brands of bubble liquid are Uncle Bubble and Gazillions of Bubbles.

243. A simple homemade recipe is 2/3 cups of Joy or Dawn dish washing soap, 1 gallon of water (distilled or tap) and 2 to 3 tablespoons of glycerin (available at most pharmacies).

244. A great resource to explore other recipes and techniques is soapbubblewikia.com.

245. Bubbles are very sensitive to environmental conditions. When working indoors, try to eliminate all air movements by turning off air conditioners.

246. Dry air can also be a problem, and some bubble artists will travel with a humidifier or hazer to put more moisture into and thicken the air where they are performing.

247. It is important to rehearse in the space and under the conditions in which you will be performing.

248. Ground covering is an important concern. After a bubble performance the stage can be left in a slippery and dangerous condition.

249. Have a tarp big enough to cover the entire performance area, and if doing walk around, be especially careful over slick surfaces like tile or polished wood.

250. In walk around situations, consider using a bubble sword that is filled with bubble liquid so a tray, that can be spilled, will not be necessary.

251. When making a large bubble big enough to encompass a child, make sure to use bubble soap liquid that pops clean and leaves very little residue.

252. Different wands are used for different sized bubbles or to produce many bubbles at once. 2 types are a tri-wand that can be used for large bubbles, and a garland wand that can be used to produce many bubbles at once.

253. Bubble artists have used tobacco smoke to fill the bubbles to make them look more visible, but most have switched to smoke machines or vaporizers to avoid the negative stigma and health consequences of using cigarettes.

254. Tom Noddy is considered the Godfather of Bubble Artists, and is a great inspiration for anyone looking to see a master of this art form at work.

255. Bubble artists will also use their bare hands to create the bubbles. Bay area bubble artist Sterling Johnson is a good example of an artist who uses this technique.

256. Make sure after a performance to wash any left-over soap residue off of your props.

257. When performing outdoors, make sure to have the wind at your back.

258. Kids can act quite chaotic and run around chasing and attempting to pop the bubbles, crowd control can be an important issue to consider. ❖

Whips

259. Always wear eye protection when learning and practicing with a bull whip.

260. The ears are another sensitive area that can hurt quite a bit when hit so consider ear protection as well in the form of a head band or head phones. This will also protect the ears from the loud sound the whip makes.

261. The two most common whips used by performers are the Bull whip and the Stock whip.

262. The two are pretty much the same, but the Stock whip has a leather hinge at the base of the handle.

263. Of the two, the Bull whip is felt to be easier to aim with. I would use that style of whip if you plan to knock a cigarette out of a volunteer's mouth. (If you decide to do this stunt, please do so with the volunteer's safety as your number one concern).

264. The end of the whip has a piece of twine that is frayed at the tip called the Cracker.

265. A whip makes a loud booming sound when cracked successfully because the end of the whip actually breaks the sound barrier moving at over 770 miles per hour.

266. When beginning, just attempt to get a softer popping sound, and wait until you improve your technique before applying the actual speed and force needed to get a true crack.

267. Start with the whip held by the handle in an upright fashion, you create a bend in the whip, and as you move your hand towards the ground the whip will wave forward causing the momentum to travel from the thicker part of the whip to the thinner part and finally to the very tip.

268. If your technique is poor, it is possible to snap off the cracker of the end of the whip, so be careful when letting an untrained person use your whip.

269. Even worse, when used incorrectly, the momentum of the whip instead of moving forward will react in a more straight up and down fashion causing the end of the whip to rise up to head height where it can very easily come back and hit the user in the face.

270. The speed of the whip allows you to cut things with the whip; common objects for this stunt include newspapers and playing cards.

271. It is much more difficult to pop a balloon with a bull whip than you think. A small fish hook can be tied into the cracker, but be careful of the additional danger this presents to the whip cracker or volunteer.

272. When knocking an object out of a person's mouth, it is very important to have the whip crack past the person. Have the fatter part of the whip strike the object, not the very tip where the cracker is.

273. Having the whip crack past the volunteer greatly reduces the danger to the volunteer, yet still allows the whip to make the loud popping sound as it passes the volunteers face. (See tip # 263).

274. If the weather is very humid a leather whip may not crack. You might consider having a nylon whip as a backup for wet conditions.

275. When not in use, keep your ropes dry and in an airtight case or bag.

276. When traveling by air be aware that whips and ropes are not allowed in your carry-on bag.

277. A lot of great Australian whip artist use whips made of Kangaroo skin. These are the most expensive type of whips.

278. A nylon whip is cheaper and won't be affected by humidity.

279. A 6 foot whip is a good length for stage performances. A 4 footer is hard to aim with for hitting targets, and very few performance spaces will have room for a 9 footer.

280. A good source for high quality whips is www.adam-winrichwhips.com

281. Try to keep the integrity of the bend in the whip when not in use, packing it in your suitcase surrounded by clothing is one good way when traveling.

282. Never bend the whip into an unnatural shape.

283. Always check the condition of the cracker (also called the popper) and where it is tied on to the whip before each performance, they will wear down over time, and you will need more force to get them to pop.

284.   The thin part of the whip where the cracker is tied to is called the "fall."

285.   Make sure your performance space has enough room so that nothing will interfere with the path of the whip. Check the floor, and the space above and behind you.

286.   Be aware of the possibility that the whip could snag or get hung up on your heel. The force of the whip getting caught could bring your whipping hand back towards your face, and I have heard of this resulting in a broken nose.

287.   Bring a backup whip and cracker if the whip is an important part of your show.

288.   The longer the cracker (1" to 2"), the louder the pop.

289.   Be careful practicing or performing on a rough surface like cement or asphalt. The whips especially the ones made of kangaroo skin can get scuffed and frayed over time.

290.   If you are using a leather whip, keep it oiled with a leather conditioner to keep it looking good, and from breaking.

291.   To see a true master of the western arts, search for Vince Bruce on YouTube. ❖

Balancing

292. When balancing an object on your face, choose the chin, forehead or the bridge of the nose. All are doable but you might find you have a preference (I personally am a forehead guy).

293. A tall object is easier to balance than a short object. For example a broom is much easier than a teaspoon.

294. If one end of the balanced object is heavier (like a pool cue), it is easier to balance if the heavier end is at the top.

295. Check out the lights above you if performing at a new venue. Lights shining directly downwards from the ceiling can be blinding and make balancing much more difficult.

296. Looking upwards into a mirror on the ceiling can be very disorienting and make the balance difficult to maintain.

297. If you will be performing balancing stunts, work to keep your neck and shoulders loose, flexible, and pain free. A crick in your neck can make it harder to get your head back far enough to balance an object comfortably.

298. Keep your eyes focused on the top of the object. Try to adjust the balance by using the upper half of your body and not by moving your feet.

299. A peacock feather can be a good first object to learn to balance. It's light weight allows you to correct the balance since it will not fall in any direction very quickly.

300. A peacock feather can also be blown through a tube high into the air (when ceiling height allows), and caught in a balance on your face or hand as it floats back to the ground.

301. If attempting to catch the launched peacock feather on your forehead, be careful of it landing in your eye.

302. If you are attempting to balance a unicycle on your chin, be careful of it slipping off and having one of the pedals strike you in the face on the way down.

303. When performing outside, consider wearing sunglasses. The sunshine can make it difficult to look up without squinting.

304. Moving clouds can also be disorienting. Always try to rehearse balancing stunts in the conditions you will be performing them in.

305. A classic gimmicked balance, is to throw up a ping pong ball and catch it in a pretend balance on your nose or forehead. This requires the ball to be tacky with rubber cement. A small additional amount on your nose or forehead can make this trick easier.

306. The ingredients in rubber cement were not meant to be applied to your face, and this is not really a very healthy trick to perform on a regular basis.

307. When kicking an object from the foot to a balance on the face (i.e. a cane from foot to chin), attempt to bring the foot up with a bent knee and lift it quite high. This will allow the object to come up straight. Try to just clear your chin, and then cushion the object with a slight downward motion as you catch it.

308. Hopping an object from chin to nose to forehead while maintaining the balance can be done with small upward motions of the upper body. Start by bending and then quickly straightening your knees.

309. Balancing a baseball cap or other borrowed hat on its brim on the bridge of your nose or forehead, and then allowing it to fall backwards landing on your head, is a nice crowd-pleasing stunt (adding a drum-roll and cymbal-crash is a good touch).

310. When balancing and juggling at the same time, always focus on maintaining the balance first. Keep your eyes looking toward the top of the balanced object, and see the juggling pattern in the bottom of your peripheral vision.

311. Before learning to juggle with a balance, it is important to be able to hold a steady balance for a good amount of time without moving your feet. ❖

Ball Spinning

312. It's important to start with a decent spinning ball. The ball should not be too light, and it should have a surface that makes it easy to grip.

313. The smaller the ball is the harder it is too learn to spin. Start with a ball about the size of a basketball or soccer ball.

314. The ball should be a little underinflated, but not so much that the audience thinks you are cheating.

315. An under-inflated ball will also have more friction and spin slower and not as long.

316. A cheap and easy ball to learn to spin with, can be made using a double or triple walled beach ball (one by itself is too light). Cut a hole around the first beach ball's nozzle big enough to stuff the second un-inflated beach ball inside, and have the second ball's nozzle stick out the hole. Inflate the inner ball.

317. The rubber soccer ball, available from Walmart during Easter time (it comes in an Easter basket), is a popular spinning ball currently being used. It can also be found on Amazon.

318. If the soccer ball is waterproofed, making it slippery, the waterproof coating can be removed with acetate.

319. A playground ball can also be modified to be a good spinning ball by sanding down the area you spin on. It is sanded down to reduce your finger's friction with the ball's bumpy surface.

320. Be aware that the area where you spin the ball can wear out, and the ball will puncture if the skin of the ball gets too thin. This is especially true if you are putting the spinning ball on a pointy stick; never use something sharp like a knife point because it could pop the ball.

321. A good point to spin the ball on can be made with the ball bearing from a spin top, because if you place a spinning ball on it there will virtually be no friction.

322. Using an angled mouth stick to place the spinning ball on, is an easy and impressive way to perform a combination trick with juggling and spinning at the same time.

323. Grip the ball with your fingertips (it should not be resting in your palm).

324. Keep your elbow tucked in to the side of your body when making the spinning motion; this will keep the ball from flying out on an angle.

325. The common direction to spin a ball is counter clockwise, and it is important that the ball spins completely parallel to the floor. If you spin it at an angle it will not stabilize when you try to catch it on your finger.

326. Give it a good sharp spin, the harder you spin it, the longer the ball will spin.

327. Having a bit of a fingernail helps. Catching it on the skin of the finger pad will cause it to slow down very quickly. You can catch it on the pad initially, but quickly transfer it to the nail to reduce friction.

328. Serious ball spinners even experiment with phony press-on nails, or allow their nails to grow out and file them to points.

329. Make sure to cushion the ball as it lands on your fingertip. Don't stab at the ball as you try to catch it. It helps to let the finger bend a little on contact to give the ball a softer landing.

330. It is very difficult to spin most balls (unless they have an extreme grip) when your hands are sweaty. Have a towel handy, or use powder to make sure your hands are dry before performing any ball spinning tricks.

331. If you are using the same ball for tricks like body rolls or neck catches, be aware that the sweat from your body can also make the ball very slippery.

332. Many balls are not made completely even, because they are made in two halves and then put together. The heavier side should be directly at the top and not the side you catch on your finger.

333. To find the heavier side of the ball, place it in a tub of water so that the heavy end will rotate to the bottom, and then mark the spot on top that you plan to spin on with a permanent marker.

334. It is good for performing to have a design on the ball that will allow the audience to see it spinning.

335. When the ball is spinning fast enough, you will only have to keep your finger upright to keep it balanced. The gyroscopic behavior of the ball will do the rest.

336. Transferring the spinning ball from your finger to a volunteer's finger or a stick the volunteer is holding is a very nice effect. It helps if the ball is spinning quite fast, and the volunteer keeps their hand still.

337. A hat or helmet with a point on top can also be used to spin a ball on.

338. If you leave a spinning ball under hot lights or in the sun, the air inside the ball will expand causing it to become full and harder to spin.

339. Placing the spinning ball on a pole to balance on your chin will not make the balance any more difficult, since the ball will remain stable till it starts to slow down.

340. Hitting the ball with short sharp slaps in the direction of the spin using your free hand can be useful to speed the ball up when it starts to slow down.

341. To perform a double ball spin where one ball spins on another on the same finger, it's easier if the bottom ball is larger and heavier.

342. Get the bottom ball spinning as fast as possible, and as quickly as you can, place the smaller ball about

one inch directly above it. As you drop the smaller ball, give it a slight spin in the same direction as the bottom ball.

343. Look where the two balls meet for the balancing point, and try to keep the bottom ball as stable as possible.

344. Give a slight upward push to the bottom ball in the direction of the free hand. This will separate the two balls and make it possible to catch one in each hand. ❖

Boomerangs

345. A good resource for indoor boomerangs is www.broadbentboomerangs.com

346. Indoor boomerangs are made of lightweight plastic and are much lighter than the outside model that is made of balsa wood.

347. Boomerangs come in left and right-handed models; so make sure to get the one that works with your dominant hand.

348. For an indoor setting the 3 or 4 wing boomerang is most likely your best option.

349. Ask for an extra thin backyard model for juggling more than one. They are lighter and have a smaller return radius.

350. Expect to need at least 25' of space to give the boomerang enough room to fly out and return.

351. Always warm up in the space you plan to perform, watch out for overhead lights and air-conditioning vents.

352. Boomerangs do partly rely on air flow, be aware that in high elevations the boomerang might not return due to the thin air.

353. Juggle 2 or more boomerangs in the shower pattern starting with the boomerangs fanned out in the non-throwing hand.

354. In addition to juggling, another impressive trick is to throw out multiple boomerangs at the same time. 3 or 4 can be thrown out at once and be caught.

355. Even one boomerang thrown out over the audience and caught in creative ways (under the leg, behind the back, etc.), can be an effective performance stunt.

356. The V shaped outdoor boomerangs come back at a very fast rate, and should be learned with caution.

357. When performing indoors, ask for the houselights to be brought up.

358. If a peg is mounted on the middle of the boomerang it can be caught spinning in your hand on your head upon its return.

359. With some practice, you can learn to throw the boomerang through a hula hoop held up by a person in the audience.

360. An outdoor boomerang can be modified to cut an apple on your head when it returns to you. Extreme caution is recommended for this stunt. ❖

Trick Roping

361. Trick roping is also referred to as lasso spinning. Supplies can be ordered from www.westernstage-props.com_

362. A good resource on trick roping is Carey Bunks "The rational guide to trick roping."

363. You can start with spot-cord - the most basic type of rope for spinning.

364. You will want different lengths for different tricks. 15' and 20' are basic lengths for tricks.

365. The length of rope you use will also depend on your height. A taller performer will use a longer rope than a shorter performer.

366. Put a knot or knob at the end of the rope above your hand. This will allow you to hold the end firmly, and easily identify where the end is without looking.

367. You will need a much longer rope for the giant loop trick, but this is a more advanced move and not a place to start.

368. You are always twisting the rope through your fingers as you spin it so that it will not kink up. Do not be surprised if you experience some cramping in your hand or wrist when you first begin.

369. Try to push the rope with your thumb as you roll it with the other fingers.

370.   In some tricks where the rope does not turn like the "butterfly" remember it's all in the wrist.

371.   You want to perform trick roping over a smooth surface.   Carpeted areas will provide too much resistance.

372.   If performing over grass, consider putting down plywood or some other type of flooring to provide a smoother performing area. Performing over grass will also leave your rope with green grass stains.

373.   If you plan to lasso a volunteer as one of your stunts make sure to practice sufficiently so as not to hit them in the head. A rope hitting someone in the face can be quite painful.

374.   Carefully coil your ropes before you put them away, or they will get kinked in weird shapes during transport. Have Velcro ties to hold the coils together.

375.   If you plan to wear boots or a cowboy hat during your act make sure to practice in the outfit you plan to use. Both these items of clothing will make certain moves more difficult.

376.   Rope tricks will take up more room than most other types of juggling or manipulation stunts. Make sure you have a sufficient performance space.

377.   It is good to learn to spin the rope with both hands and in both directions to develop you overall skill and control.

378. Accomplished ropers will often add a bit of weight to the point where the rope meets the loop (the Honda) you can do this by taping pennies or nickels to the sides of the rope.

379. The extra weight created by weighting the rope will give you better control. Since the Honda area is where you will be focusing most of your attention.

380. For ticks like the Big Loop or The Texas Skip (where you jump through the rope from side to side) you will want to put a "Burner" (a thin piece of leather or metal) on the Honda to eliminate friction.

381. Consider trying a rope with a nylon core it will make the rope softer but it will be more consistent in different conditions.

382. Try a nylon indoor climbing rope, it doesn't make the tricks any easier but it will never wear out, and is not affected by humidity or other variable conditions.

383. With most ropes you will want to replace them every 3-4 months. They will go through a process where they will need to be broken in, then are perfect, and then become more difficult to use do to wear and tear.

384. The big loop takes a lot of energy and strength on the shoulder and elbow. Listen to your body and if you start to experience any pain, take some time off so you don't make it worse. ❖

Ping pong ball juggling

385.   It is easier to learn with a ball that is a proper size for your mouth.

386.   The current standard for competition is 40mm which is a bit too large for most jugglers; try to find the older 38mm ping pong balls on the internet since they are no longer carried in sporting goods stores.

387.   The three star balls are better for mouth juggling. A heavier ball is easier to control than a lighter ball.

388.   Cheap ping pong balls that only have one star usually have a noticeable seam, are too light, and can be slightly uneven making them more difficult to use.

389.   You will want to keep the balls wet when practicing or performing. It is good to keep the balls slightly slick and not have them stick to your lips or inside of your mouth.

390.   If keeping them in water, change the water often and keep the balls in a clean sanitary environment. Make sure the floor where you practice or perform is not dirty and dusty.

391.   Try to bend the head back into a position that brings the mouth parallel and allows you to spit the ball straight up. Do this mostly by bending the neck to rest against the shoulders, and not from arching the lower back.

392.   It is helpful if the neck is flexible, trying to get your head into the proper position with a sore or stiff neck makes the trick much more difficult.

393.   Try for a high spit at first, this will give you more time and help you work on the control you will need to learn two or more balls.

394.   After spitting one ball high, have the second ball held in your hand at face level and quickly feed it into your mouth to start the two ball juggling pattern.

395.   Juggle two balls in a parallel column pattern with your head moving from side to side to keep the balls next to each other. Keep them even with the second ball being spit when the first one reaches its apex.

396.   Keep your tongue level with your lower lip, blocking the bottom teeth and creating a soft landing place for the balls.

397.   Experiment with keeping one foot next to, but slightly behind the other foot. This allows you to move more freely in all directions.

398.   Putting one ball in each cheek and facing the crowd looking like a chipmunk never fails to get a laugh.

399.   It is a good skill to learn how to keep two balls inside your mouth (not in the cheeks) one above the other. Try to start by spitting one ball while one remains in your mouth.

400. Think about your hand position. Try learning with your hands on the hips to avoid an awkward position with the arms.

401. Have different colored balls to help with the visibility (white and orange are the two most common colors). Ping pong balls are small and you want to make sure the audience can see them well against the background you are performing in front of.

402. Just like with balancing make sure to practice under the conditions you will be performing. Staring up into a light that blinds you can make this trick nearly impossible to do.

403. Make sure there is an even and adequate stage lighting covering the space above you where the balls will be flying. Having them go from the light into the darkness and back into the light can increase the difficulty of the trick.

404. Windy conditions and bright sun when working outdoors can greatly affect this trick and make it much more difficult.

405. Be careful of the choking hazard that can result when trying this trick with any object smaller than a 38mm ping pong ball.

406. When not in use, keep your ping pong balls in a container that will prevent them from being crushed or dented in transport. ❖

Straight jacket escape

407. Straight jackets for performing escapes can be bought at specialty magic suppliers like www.Real-straightjackets.com, or fetish stores like www.Monkeydungeon.com.

408. Expect to pay at least $250.00 for a jacket that looks like a real restraint. Cheaper ones can be found at costume stores, but they look too light weight and flimsy to make the escape look impressive.

409. A straight jacket escape is not a magic trick, but gaffed jackets that allow you to hold a strap inside the sleeve to create extra slack can be purchased.

410. In a gaffed (rigged or fixed to be made easier) straight jacket, the shoulder seam will also be made wider so your elbow can get free with less effort.

411. The common way to create slack when being tied up is to hold your breath, puff out your chest and hold your arms stiffly and slightly away from your body.

412. Be careful that they stage or the shoes you are wearing are not slippery. You want to have a good footing. Falling while your arms are restrained can be dangerous since you cannot break your fall.

413. Be careful you are not too close to the edge of the stage because you will be doing a lot of flailing around, and when the arm sleeve is coming over your head your vision will be obscured.

414.   Choosing your volunteers wisely is an important part of the escape, try to choose people who will follow your instructions and not try to mess you up or hurt you by being too rough.

415.   Escaping from a straight jacket is a very physical stunt. Be careful not to over exert yourself, pull a muscle or injure your lower back.

416.   If you have not done the trick for a while or have gained a bit of weight since you last attempted it, don't be surprised when it is more difficult than you remember.

417.   Have the volunteer (or volunteers) do the back buckles first, then your arms, and finally the crotch. Make sure your strong arm is on top.

418.   Using only one volunteer and having them work quickly can cut down on the possibility of being messed with. It is important that when you get the sleeves tied behind you that yours arms won't be pinned by the straps going through the back loops. This would prevent you from being able to bring your arms over your head.

419.   If you work as a duo, consider having one performer supervise while the other one is being tied up. This will prevent you being restrained in a way that you cannot escape from.

420.   In addition to puffing out your chest, secretly pinch the front of the jacket to be able to create slack after your arms are tied.

421. If you are wearing a lavalier microphone it will be muffled by the jacket. A headset mic will be difficult to wear, and could be damaged when you bring your arm over your head to escape.

422. If you plan to speak during the escape have a stand mic available or have one of the volunteers hold the mic in front of your mouth.

423. You will not be able to wear glasses, a hat, or a toupee, since they will probably be knocked off during the escape. (I have not seen it done, but I imagine having a hairpiece that is knocked off seemingly by accident could be quite funny).

424. One main source of comedy in the escape, is the tying of the crotch strap. Making the volunteer uncomfortable, and having them reach for it several times while you swing it out of their reach seems quite standard.

425. The jacket should be a washable material like canvas. Escaping is sweaty work especially if you do outdoor shows. You will want to be able to clean your jacket (a leather one might look cool, but dry cleaning it will be expensive).

426. To do the escape push your strong arm towards the opposite shoulder, as you keep the other arm close to your body, this creates the slack necessary to pull the arm over top over your head.

427. Use your teeth to unbuckle the arm strap, but if you use chains in addition to the straight jacket be very careful, especially if the volunteers looped the chain over your head.

428. Some performers will claim that they need to dislocate their shoulder to do the escape. This is just a part of the patter and no actual physical pain or freakish ability needs to be employed.

429. You will want to flail around and make the escape look very dramatic, dropping to the ground and rolling around can be one effective way to make the escape appear more difficult.

430. Be careful that the volunteers or other audience members are not too close to you as you wave around your arms. Striking someone with a strap or buckle in the face would be something to avoid at all costs.

431. Be prepared to feel claustrophobic at first, it is advisable to learn this skill with an experienced performer, and always have someone nearby to let you out in case of emergencies.

432. Most performers will set a time limit (for example how long it took Houdini) and attempt to beat it. Get out of the jacket at the very last second for the most dramatic finish possible.

433. Be careful at the end since you will be rushing. If the jacket is tight, you may experience some bruising on your outer arms as you struggle to get out.

434. An audience countdown of the last 10 seconds can help add to the drama. Consider slamming the jacket down when you have finally escaped and striking a dramatic pose. ❖

Rope walking

435.   When performing this stunt on the streets, make sure your valuables including your money bag are safely stowed away during your performance.

436.   You should wear soft thin soled shoes to be able to feel the rope, but make sure the bottoms are not too slippery to have good traction.

437.   Tight wire is thinner, doesn't stretch, and looks more impressive, but is much more difficult to rig and transport than a slack rope.

438.   One inch Manila offers good solid support for a slack rope, but not for a tight rope since it will stretch.

439.   Slack line is a popular option because of its springier trampoline effect.

440.   A slack rope is difficult to do on the street because you will need a portable rig or existing structures to tie off to.

441.   You might also face complaints if you tie off to existing structures or buildings because of the fear of property damage or liability issues.

442.   A portable rigging for a tight rope that requires a winch will probably weigh at least a couple of hundred pounds.

443.   For juggling it is best to use the slack rope since you will have a steadier static balance when you are at the bottom of the rope's pendulum arc.

444. You will balance on one foot to juggle, and it is possible with practice to spin a ring on the other leg.

445. A portable rig for a slack rope will be much lighter because it will not require a winch.

446. A unicycle used to balance on the rope has no tire, and you will want the rope to fit snugly inside the rim so there is no room for side to side movement.

447. The unicycle balances in one place on the rope, you do not need to idle like you do on the ground.

448. If you want volunteers to hold the rope consider how much you weigh and the strain that it will put on them.

449. You will need at least 4 strong people per side to hold an average size 160 pound person.

450. To get four volunteers on each side you are looking at a rope of around 25 feet, if you plan to put knots in it for hand holds it might be a bit longer.

451. As opposed to a tug of war where you will want the strongest people at the end, you will want to have your two biggest volunteers in the spots closest to you on each side.

452. The two closest to you will be your main support while all the rest will be adding tension.

453. You can even use children at the very ends of the rope; this can be funny since people in the audience may assume this is where the most strength is needed.

454. The two closest volunteers will also establish the height of the rope, since it will be where their arms hang down to. It is helpful if these two are close to the same height.

455. Make sure the rope is of a soft material and consider adding knots so that the volunteers will have easier hand holds.

456. Gloves for the volunteers will not be necessary if the rope is soft enough, but if you want to give out a couple pairs don't forget it's the two closest volunteers to the performer who are doing most of the work.

457. Keep yourself centered between the volunteers. This way the stress will be equal on both sides.

458. If you plan to juggle dangerous items while on the rope (knives, torches etc.), make sure there is enough space in front of you to provide a safe area for the entire pattern.

459. If you drop a prop, try to do it to the side and not straight forward. Remember, the volunteers will have their hands full and will not be able to protect themselves from falling objects.

460. Once you get up on the rope, keep it quick. Never forget the strain the volunteers are under. Be considerate to the effort they are making to help you with your show.

461. For the sake of time, do your comedy and build up first, and then have the volunteers hold you up just for the length of your trick.

462. The tension of the rope will vary and fluctuate if the volunteers laugh at your jokes or get tired. So be prepared to adjust to the variable nature of the balance.

463. The volunteers at the end may shift around to see you since they will be blocked by the people in front of them, and this can cause the rope to move.

464. Be careful when jumping off the rope especially if you do it many times a day or the ground underneath you is hard and uneven.

465. The adrenaline that pumps through you during a show can mask the pain that you will experience later, so pace yourself and try to avoid jumping off the rope if you can lower yourself instead and hop down.

466. If you find yourself losing your balance, try to hop off one side and don't fall with the rope between your legs, as this can cause serious pain or injury.

467. Keep your shoes in good condition, and buy new ones if they are falling apart or losing traction.

468. If you fall forward, try to bring your arms together and cushion yourself to protect your crotch and face from hitting the rope.

469. Try to set up the rope so you will not be walking while facing into the sun or bright stage lights. You want to keep your eyes up and forward, and being blinded by light will make balancing more difficult.

470. A parasol or small umbrella can help with balance and control, but can make it more difficult to stay on the rope under windy conditions.

471. Panels can be cut into the parasol to allow the wind to blow through it.

472. Don't perform with people under the rope, the chance of injuring a spectator if you fall is not worth the risk.

473. Be careful if the rigging were to come loose or snap that the audience is a safe distance away.

474. Always test the strength of a structure you are tying off to. Also, understand that conditions can change, so make sure to test them each time you set up.

475. If tying around a tree use two-by-fours and carpet to keep the pressure from gouging into the tree trunk.

476. If the bark on a tree is damaged all the way around it can kill the tree, since a tree's circulatory system is right beneath the bark.

477. Be careful if you plan to have juggling props thrown to you on the rope since your range of motion will be compromised by the need to maintain your balance.

478. Make sure any volunteers you use to hold the rope don't have any back or other health issues that will be a problem when supporting your weight.

479.   Be versatile, know when the rope cannot be used and another trick might be necessary to substitute for it.

480.   It is not always possible especially in a smaller show to get enough volunteers up on stage to hold the rope, and you don't want to have to bail on a show if that is your only finale, so have another option available. ❖

Street shows

6 of the best pitches (street performance spots) in the U.S.A.

Pearl Street Mall - Boulder Colorado, Jackson Square - New Orleans, Pier 39 - San Francisco (my home pitch), Harbor Place- Baltimore, Key West - Florida, Nathanial Hall - Boston.

481. Check to see what audition process or permits are required before performing in a new spot.

482. An area where street performance takes place is called a "pitch."

483. Some pitches limit the use of dangerous props (fire, knives, tall unicycles), so check to see what the restrictions are.

484. The same is true for amplification; not all pitches allow you to use a mic or recorded music.

485. Church Street in Burlington Vermont is good on the weekends. To join the street program contact churchstmarketplace@gmail.com

486. At Pier 39, acts are auditioned (contact Scotty Meltzer for information scottm@comedyindustries. com) and a monthly meeting is held to divvy up the available slots. Performance insurance is required. Benches, a backstage area, and a sound system are provided (must have own mic).

487. At Pearl Street Mall acts are required to have a permit (free) which you need to apply for 48 hours before

performing) Performers work on a first come first serve basis and rotate so everyone can get a show. No amps allowed, and you must have performer's insurance.

488. Harbor Place holds auditions once a year to join their street program, they have their own permit so you are not required to get an additional one, amps are allowed and there are no prop restrictions. Performers are given a 3 hour window that they do not have to share. Performer's Insurance is required (good idea to have anyways).

489. The most successful Street performers (financially) usually find a way to get up high (Tall unicycle, standing on a volunteer's shoulder's, etc.) to have greater visibility to the largest sized audience possible. Especially with their final routine.

490. The more people who can see and hear you, the more people who are likely to give you money.

491. Be clear with your speech and language. Many pitches attract tourists who may not speak English as their first language.

492. Some words are more universal in different languages, like saying "applause" versus the English "clap."

493. A rope can be a useful for creating a performance space, laid out on the ground in a semi-circle. It can establish where you want your front row of spectators to sit or stand.

494. A rope is one more large item to carry, also consider a stage outline using chalk, water line, or small cones. Etc.

495. Water poured-out in a thin line can be a good choice to mark your performance boundary because it will evaporate and leave no trace, but be careful when using chalk. Clean up after you are done because some pitches consider the chalk marks to be a form of graffiti and don't like you to leave markings on the pitch area.

496. The rope can create a barrier that you might find cumbersome or prevent you from going into the audience on a unicycle.

497. Consider starting with the rope and removing it after the core crowd has been created.

498. Kids will often find the rope interesting to play with and can be distracting to your show.

499. If you can get people to sit down in the front, it will allow more people to see and create a strong core audience.

500. Taking out a bill and putting it in your hat during your hat speech can be helpful for the non- English speakers in your audience to know what you want them to do at the end of the show.

501. Making noise and yelling to attract people to your show is called "hawking the crowd."

502. If working a street festival with multiple pitches, it is a good idea if your act is portable and easy to set up and tear down.

503. Always be aware of how much weather conditions can hurt your hat. Better to end a show early than to have your crowd flee if it starts to rain.

504. Don't be afraid to mention the amount you want as a tip, and never ask for change.

505. An average street show runs between 20 to 45 minutes in length.

506. Consider the conditions when determining the proper length for your show. On hot days, you might want to make the show shorter so you don't wear out the amount of time the crowd can comfortably watch you.

507. It certain situations you might not to want to start out too big or too aggressive. It can be a good idea to try to match the energy of the performance space and then to elevate it to show level.

508. Before performing find out if a permit is necessary and if there are any restrictions (i.e. no torches, no amplified music, etc.).

509. THE STREET IS NO PLACE FOR THE TIMID.

510. Use your pre-show activities, such as warming up or setting out your props, to build a sense of anticipation.

511. I find that doing a trick with a child volunteer is a good way to create interest in what you are doing at the beginning of your show, and if the child is with a large group or family it's even better.

512. Doing tricks that are loud and noisy (i.e. shaker cups, whip cracking, etc.) can help you attract attention.

513. Some performers will use a horn, drum, bugle or other loud instrument to draw focus.

514. Get the initial core audience to help you attract a crowd with their screams and applause.

515. A small crowd can help to attract a bigger crowd.

516. At a festival with multiple pitches, use the traffic flow that results from the end of someone else's show to help gather a crowd, but don't ever step on another performers' hat pass.

517. Be aware a crowd that has already just seen a show and tipped might be harder to get money from.

518. Be aware if a group at your show (school group, bus tour, etc.), might have to leave all at once before the show ends.

519. Starting with new people can create a stronger experience and give the audience less to compare with.

520. If someone has no money they still can post pictures on Facebook, or do something else that could be a benefit for you.

521. Start strong, end strong!

522. Just because you are a street artist doesn't mean you have to dress like a bum.

523. Even a comfortable outfit of shorts and a t-shirt can be clean and color coordinated.

524. I have heard Penn of Penn and Teller say that dressing well on the street was one of the reasons he did very well with tips.

525. If you wear your costume into Walmart and nobody stares, it's not a costume.

526. Have something you wear or personal style that helps you stand-out and separates you from the audience.

527. Take enough risks with your own or your audience's safety, and sooner or later someone is going to get hurt. Especially doing multiple shows in a day.

528. A street performer I knew used to finish his show with a 22 foot unicycle ride around the crowd. He fell one time and broke both his ankles. After he healed he resumed performing with a 10 footer as his final trick, and realized he only made about $10.00 less per show. Know what is worth risking your life for and what isn't.

529. A good street show is like a story where the audience has a strong interest to wait till it's over to see how it ends. That is why so many performers will hype their final trick during the course of their show.

530. If your street show has sections that have definite endings, this will give the crowd a chance to leave if they feel they have seen enough. Think of your show as a complete story, not a collection of individual chapters.

531. Keeping a prop out in plain view (tall unicycle, 3 chainsaws, etc.) that has the audience thinking "I can't wait to see that" is a good way to have them stay till the end of the show.

532. The last trick should be strong enough to ask for tips even if the crowd has seen nothing else.

533. If you give a volunteer something that can be broken, don't be surprised when one of them actually does break it (especially kids).

534. Never let anyone try anything that they could hurt themselves on like a unicycle or Rolla-Bolla even before or after the show.

535. Don't forget to drink a lot of water, and wear sunscreen when doing shows outdoors.

536. Consider giving a volunteer a prize of money for their time on stage. This can be a good way to re-enforce the idea that the performer expects to be tipped at the end of the show.

537. You never know who might be in your crowd, so keep it clean when working in a family friendly environment. Getting complaints is not a good way to create good will, and it will affect your ability to work at a pitch.

538. If you get into an argument with a local business, you are bound to lose because management usually considers street performers less important than vendors. Be courteous.

539. Make sure your crowd doesn't block or interfere with any local businesses by preventing access to their shop or stall.

540. Also make sure your sound level is not annoying to the local establishments. You will definitely get complaints if the vendors feel you're interfering with their ability to conduct business.

541. Try to consider everyone in the pitch environment as being part of a team, and always try to work towards the mutual benefit of the entire group.

542. Keep a close eye on your props so people can't walk off with them. Working with other performers who will watch your back is a good idea in sketchy situations.

543. Keep your props together and close to you. Don't leave them randomly lying around you on the pitch as your show progresses. At the end, when people crowd in to give you tips, they can be stepped on or easily stolen.

544. You want to keep the pace tight and the show moving. Street show audiences have a notoriously short attention span.

545. When someone really doesn't want to help you in your act, don't try to force them. Just move on and pick someone else.

546. If you pick a volunteer and they turn out to be a problem (drunk, obnoxious, etc.), there is no rule that says you have to use them. Send them back into the crowd and get someone else.

547. If replacing a volunteer, try to make it seem like it is a part of you show, and not just a slam on the volunteer.

548. Be careful when picking volunteers who might have physical or mental disabilities that will prevent them from achieving success on stage.

549. Just because someone looks strong and sturdy doesn't mean that they might not have problems with their backs or knees. Be careful with any stunt that requires lifting or supporting your body weight (i.e. hanging on someone as they help you mount an unicycle or standing on their shoulders).

550. If the stunt is physically demanding, ask the volunteer if they have any medical conditions that might prevent them from performing it.

551. One venue I know of will no longer allow performers to use volunteers, because one time a volunteer brought up on stage claimed they were injured during a stunt, and tried to sue the club.

552. Never forget how your careless actions can affect the entire pitch and the other performers' ability to earn money.

553. If you use volunteers, it can be a good idea to scout the crowd before the show starts for likely candidates.

554. Try to bring up a volunteer for a stunt who you feel will provide the most comedy potential based on what you want them to do.

555. A good act has no trouble getting volunteers, but nobody wants to be in a show that's going badly.

556. People in the audience should want to do what the chosen volunteer ends up doing. If you treat your volunteer disrespectfully, you will have trouble getting others to help you later in the show.

557. Be very careful when deciding whether or not your want to use a heckler or over-enthusiastic member of the crowd as a volunteer in your show.

558. Audiences usually feel more protective towards female volunteers. Don't come across mean or the crowd may turn against you.

559. Let the crowd know you depend solely upon them for your livelihood.

560. Inform the crowd you'll be passing your hat after the show, before you perform your final trick. Some performers suggest mentioning this fact several times during the show as well.

561. Some performers will pass the hat before the final trick. This seems to be a common tactic of breakdance groups and more aggressive street performers, but this only works in certain situations, and I don't recommend it for most acts.

562. If your finale requires you to be a distance away from the audience, (for example the top of a long incline rope walk or otherwise encumbered), consider passing the hat before the final stunt.

563. At some pitches you are not allowed to actually physically pass the hat. You are required to have a bucket or other type of receptacle on the ground that people will come up to and drop the money in to. Always make sure you follow the rules established by the pitch management in this regard.

564. See a lot of different shows and try to work a lot of different pitches. Sometimes one pitch will breed similar style shows because that is what works at that location.

565. For bigger tips, it can help to end the show with something the audience thinks is dangerous.

566. If you have to push the money in your hat down to make room for more, you need a bigger hat. Also consider using larger tip bucket, basket, or even a pillow-case for larger crowds.

567. Sometimes when the audience sees a full hat they feel as if you have gotten enough already, and will use that as a reason not to give.

568. If you do multiple volunteer stunts in your show try to bring up a variety of different type of people, if you don't you might hear about the lack of diversity in your show from the crowd.

569. Having an item that you will include and give away with a bigger tip (Lanyards, postcards, etc.) can be

a very effective way to make more money for your show.

570. One street gig I have heard of (Virginia Beach) won't allow you to pass the hat, but will allow you to accept donations by having an item to sell in exchange for the show.

571. Having contact information on these items is a good way to get follow up bookings.

572. It also helps to have contact information visible while you perform. This could take the form of a banner, or simply your act's name and website address on your prop case.

573. Take advantage of social media to get additional promotion from your shows, have people twitter about you, post pictures, etc.

574. Make sure your name and contact info is in all pictures posted to social media if possible.

575. People in the crowd will judge how much to give by example. Try to collect a large tip first or early in your hat pass, and then thank the person for their generous contribution.

576. Thank everyone who gives, but keep the jokes going while collecting.

577. Make sure people know where you are when you pass the hat, don't get lost in the crowd. It helps if everyone can still see and hear you while you collect.

578. Be inconspicuous when counting your hat money or putting it away. Always keep your money bag in a safe secure location.

579. If working in a duo, and you feel uncomfortable leaving the other person unattended with the money bag, maybe that's a good sign that you shouldn't be partners.

580. It pays to be paranoid! Be careful when packing up and leaving your street performing area, especially if you are carrying a large amount of cash.

581. Bring a paper bag for each show with the show number written on it. That way, when you count the money at the end of the day, you can trace how each show went as far as the hat goes.

582. Remember a favorite Raspyni Brothers motto: "If we're there and the money's there, let's leave together."

583. Try to get the most out of a good day, street show conditions can change quickly. You might only have so many days where everything lines up in your favor so make the most of those days when you can.

584. Also know when to call it quits. When you get too tired or lose the focus needed to do a good show, it might be a good idea to pack it up and not risk injury or doing something that could impact your ability to come back to the pitch on another day.

585. The wind can be a factor, especially in juggling shows, be extra careful when using light props such as ping pong balls or rings.

586. If the weather looks iffy (rain clouds), make sure you have something to cover your props with and a place to store them where they will not get wet.

587. Even when doing street festivals where a sound system will be provided, it never hurts to bring your own small battery operated system in case of emergencies (power outage, faulty system, etc.).

588. The street can be a good place to get experience and develop an act, but be careful not to end up with a product that can only work on the street unless that is your main goal.

589. It is harder to do subtle humor on the street where you don't have the same focus or lack of distractions that you have in a theatre.

590. Protect your voice. If you scream through too many shows, you will end up sounding like a bad carnival barker with a raspy ruined voice in the long run.

591. Don't smoke! There is nothing about this habit that will help you or your show.

592. Working street performing festivals can be a great way to see many different acts, and spend time hanging out with your fellow performers.

593. A great resource to hear street performers tell their stories and learn from their experiences is the "Stories From the Pitch" podcast that can be found at buskerhalloffame.com.

594. A great resource for information about busking festivals worldwide can be found at www. buskercentral.com. (Busker is another term for street performer).

595. Street performing can be hot, sweaty work. Consider bringing a change of clothes for after performances, and for the journey back to your lodgings.

596. Street festivals in their first year can have more logistic and technical problems than established festivals. Ask how many years a festival has been running before agreeing to perform there.

597. It is very helpful to ask a performer who has appeared at the festival before to give you input on the most desirable pitches and times to perform.

598. Be careful that nothing is scheduled that can interfere with your show. Parades, fireworks, or a loud band starting up are all examples of difficult distractions to overcome.

599. Wear comfortable shoes and consider using orthopedic inserts to prevent soreness after a long day of walking to and from the pitch, and being on your feet all day.

600. Make sure you wear a sunscreen that won't sting your eyes if you get sweat in them. ❖

Cruise Ships

601. Most cruise lines are booked through cruise ship agencies.

602. Three of the biggest agencies are: Bramson (www.bramson.com), Don Casino productions (www.dcptalent.com), and Spotlight entertainment (www.spolightentertainment.com). Application forms and booking requirements can be found on their websites.

603. If they are interested in an exclusive contract, you will agree to book all cruise contracts through them. You will agree to not contact any other cruise line yourself or go through other agencies to book work.

604. The longer and more expensive the cruise is, the older the passengers tend to be. (They are the only ones who can afford it, and have the free time to be off work).

605. Cruise ship audiences can vary greatly depending on the time of year and the cruise line. Knowing the type of crowd you will be performing for will help you customize your material for the best result.

606. It is very important to make a great first impression. Make sure you are ready and can do a good job before accepting your first contract.

607. A lot of first time performers are asked to work over the holidays as a try out when the regular acts want to have a break. (Christmas, Thanksgiving, etc.).

608. Before you accept a long cruise ship contract, make sure you aren't prone to seasickness or claustrophobia.

609. If you can take a cruise as a passenger first, it is a good way to see if cruise life is for you, and will give you an idea of the quality of cruise ship entertainment on that particular line.

610. If you are claustrophobic, be warned – cruise ship cabins can be quite small and an inside cabin will have no windows.

611. Just because an old crowd is not noisy or overly responsive, doesn't mean they're not enjoying the show. Do not berate them for their lack of response.

612. When performing in front of an older crowd be sure you are talking slowly enough and clearly enough for everyone to understand you.

613. Cruise ships like you to use modern up to date music, but make sure your choices are appropriate for the age range and sensibilities of the audience.

614. Make sure the volume of the music won't upset older passengers.

615. If asked to perform in a cruise ship lounge, and not the showroom, don't be surprised if the ceiling is less than 12 feet high.

616. In heavy seas, cruise ship showrooms have a tendency to rock back and forth. This makes some tricks (especially ones that require balance) more difficult.

617.   It is not uncommon for the juggler to be asked to perform when the seas are deemed too rough for the dancers to work safely.

618.   If you can, use the ship rocking to your advantage to add comedy to your routines or make an easy trick seem more difficult to perform.

619.   Just because you are going someplace nice, doesn't always mean you will get a chance to enjoy it. You might be asked to rehearse during port days, or not have enough time to really enjoy a new location.

620.   If you are disembarking the ship in a nice locale, you might want to arrange to stay a few extra days before flying home.

621.   Your offstage behavior counts just as much as what you do on stage. Always be courteous and polite, especially in public areas.

622.   Each cruise ship line grants different status to the performers. On some, you are not allowed to take advantage of some features (the hot tub or gambling to name a couple), and you might find yourself staying in the crew area as opposed to a passenger cabin.

623.   Some cruise lines like you to use the show band, so bring musical charts if you have them. This seems to be getting rarer.

624.   Make sure you have all the promotional material you need for your show. All photos are in the proper format and are professionally done.

625. A "gobo" can add a nice professional touch. (A gobo is a stencil that can be put over a light to shine a logo on the front curtain before the show).

626. Some cruise lines will allow you to sell merchandise after your show or in the gift shops. If you are interested in doing that, make sure to check what that particular ship's policies on sales are.

627. The dress code on some ships can be quite formal (they will even have specific formal nights), so don't forget to bring nice clothes if necessary (i.e. coat and tie, slacks, dress shoes, etc.).

628. Check with the cruise line if you can bring a guest. There is often a small fee required, but it can be a nice way to vacation with family or friends.

629. Cruising by yourself can be quite lonely; it is often a good idea to buddy up with the other performers on the ship to make the time pass more enjoyably.

630. Be ready to perform at least two twenty-five minutes sets. (The time you need for a ship can vary from 8 minutes if you come on as part of a production show to as much as 90 total minutes of material over multiple shows). Make sure you know what is expected of you.

631. It is very important to do the time you are asked to do. There is a specific schedule for the day and if you go too long or too short it might throw off other activities.

632. A member of the cruise staff will be there at the end of your show to thank you and get you off stage. They might only get there 5 minutes before you are supposed to end. If you finish early and they are not there to see you off, it will definitely look bad.

633. A wireless lavalier microphone should be used if you do any verbal material. They are provided and you are not required to bring your own.

634. Performers are often re-hired on the strength of the passenger's comment cards. Off stage be friendly and engage with the passengers in an open and courteous manner. Even if you have a great show, being rude and getting a bad comments will make it difficult for you to get repeat bookings.

635. Bring your passport (check to make sure it's up to date), and at least two 8" x 10" promotional photos.

636. Having a porthole and being above the water-line makes your cabin a lot more comfortable. If you are very lucky or on a premium line you might have a balcony with a sliding door. (Having fresh air in your cabin is a real plus).

637. Make sure to attend all required safety meetings and meet with immigration officials at the scheduled time.

638. If you drink, make sure to do so responsibly and don't over indulge. Check to see if there is a crew bar and never appear drunk in public.

639. Internet access can be expensive on the ship, and a connection is not always available. Have someone who can handle your business, if necessary while you are away. ❖

Practicing and Perfecting your Routines

640. Write out your comedy material, and when you practice, say the lines out loud.

641. Practice with people who inspire you. People who truly excel don't resent excellence in others.

642. Videotape your practice sessions and as many shows as possible.

643. Juggling is a physical activity. Work on your strength, flexibility, and aerobic conditioning.

644. Run through your routines under simulated performance conditions. Wear your costume and use the same props you'll be using during your performance.

645. Sometimes the magic is in the eraser. What you take out can be as important to a routine as what you leave in.

646. Don't expect to improve every day, with every performance, or at the same rate that someone else does.

647. The quality and consistency of the time you spend practicing is more important then the quantity of time.

648. You can buy all the props you want, but you can't pay someone to practice for you.

649. Be your own biggest fan, but also be your own biggest critic.

650. Listen to, and learn from the audience. They are right every time.

651. As a juggler, never teach yourself that it's okay to drop. When you practice, do so in a deliberate fashion on tricks that are challenging, but within your abilities.

652. Learn alternate ways to pick up fallen props, including using your feet.

653. You might not get paid every day, but there's no reason you can't work every day.

654. If a funny situation or line occurs spontaneously during a performance, figure out a way to repeat it every show.

655. Remember, it doesn't always have to be your way to be the best way.

656. Just because you don't think someone is as good as you, doesn't mean they can't teach you something.

657. Don't be afraid to nit-pick.

658. Practice what you're NOT good at.

659. Think of your act like it's a shark swimming through the water. If it stops moving forward, it will die.

660. Just because a joke gets a laugh, doesn't mean it's a good joke or that it belongs in your routine. Think of the tone and image you are trying to present.

661. When it comes to performance, character can be just as important as technique, so make sure to give that proper focus and attention.

662. Positive visualization can be used as a helpful tool in perfecting your routines.

663. Be aware of any repetitive speech patterns, such as saying "like," or "you know," "here you go," "alright," etc., or physical tics you might have.

664. Learn from your mistakes, and don't make the same mistake twice.

665. Put as much time and effort into the elements you add to your juggling routine (i.e., comedy or dance) as you do into the juggling itself.

666. For a quick lesson in the importance of perfection, practice juggling brand new silicone balls on top of a steep hill.

667. Break down complex or combination tricks into easier to learn individual parts.

668. Try to work both hands equally.

669. Remember, sometimes the most difficult stunts are not the ones the audience appreciates the most.

670. During a show, there's nothing wrong with using a hidden gimmick to make a trick easier to perform.

671. You can be like a rocket and take it easy, reaping the benefits after a big burst of creative energy, but you can't coast from the start.

672. Don't over train!

673. Treat your props like tools, not toys, even if the prop is a toy.

674. Be generous with your talents. Benefit shows are a good place to work on new material.

675. Take classes in skills that will help your performing ability (i.e. acting, comedy writing, dance, mime, etc.).

676. Stock up on particular props that you like because they might be difficult to find at a later date.

677. Work on the dexterity of your fingers. Piano playing, baton twirling, and coin manipulation can all be helpful.

678. Get feedback on your routines from both performers and non-performers.

679. Be a mentor – sometimes the best way to learn is by teaching someone else.

680. When juggling, try starting even numbers of objects with your left hand, odd numbers with your right.

681. New props (especially silicone balls) can get slippery. Break them in during rehearsal before using them in a show.

682. When practicing, harness the power of music to help energize you and stimulate your creativity.

683. There is nothing wrong with a routine not being funny, unless of course, it's <u>supposed</u> to be funny.

684. Practice, practice, practice! ❖

Creating Routines

685. Be original. If you can't be original, at least use old ideas in a new and original way.

686. The best way to come up with a good idea is to come up with a lot of ideas.

687. Implement an idea as soon as possible, as you'll learn alot by bringing it into reality, even in its most basic form.

688. It's hard to replace someone else's joke once you find out that it works in your routine. Try not to rely on stock material.

689. Don't be afraid to move your original jokes around from one routine to another. I call this technique, "stealing from myself."

690. When doing a television spot, try to mine your entire show to see which of your best jokes will fit in the routine you decide to do.

691. Don't forget the foreign market. Try translating your verbal routines into other languages. Think about having a verbal and non-verbal version of each of your acts.

692. Just because you think something is impossible, doesn't mean it can't be done.

693. Trust your own instincts. If someone is going to be wrong, it might as well be you.

694. Learn and get inspiration from other art forms.

695. Brainstorm with other variety performers.

696. Don't let the lack of an idea on how to present a skill prevent you from working on the skill itself.

697. Look through hardware stores, toy shops and sporting goods stores for ideas and inspiration.

698. Watch silent movies, especially Chaplin, Lloyd and Keaton.

699. Combine your art form with some form of locomotion (ice skating, unicycling, etc.).

700. Exploit your already existing abilities or physical attributes.

701. If you have a large prop and find out you can do without it, you will eventually end up leaving it at home.

702. Substitute common props with ones that are more unusual.

703. Never say "no" to yourself. You will get enough rejection from others, so don't jump the gun.

704. "Be so good they can't ignore you"- Steve Martin.

705. Have a show-biz role model (mine is Steve Martin).

706. Develop directed thought, and depth-of-thought. Focus on a particular problem and explore all of the possible solutions.

707. Work on a variety of skills. It's hard to put together a 45-minute show if you only concentrate on one or two props. ❖

Before the show

708. Leave early! Give yourself plenty of time to get where you need to go, set up your props, and scope out the situation.

709. Print out your introduction and your light and sound cues.

710. Never depend on second-hand-information. Go to the source for important facts, like location and showtimes.

711. When arriving at a new venue, call to arrange someone to meet you outside to take you to the dressing room, especially if you will be bringing in props.

712. I prefer to get a 50% deposit and the balance of the check due at arrival prior to the performance.

713. If a long term gig is to be "Pro-rated" (paid by the day), make sure to ask if that includes any travel days, rehearsals or days off.

714. Don't stereotype venues (i.e. all comedy clubs like dirty material, etc.).

715. If you are doing any bounce juggling, check the stage floor for dead spots.

716. For safety sake, look to see how close the audience will be sitting to your performance space.

717. If you use volunteers in your show, make sure they will have easy access to the stage.

718. Make sure your clothing is loose enough for you to move comfortably.

719. Keep your fingernails short and clean.

720. Have a rehearsal whenever possible. Run through your act with the lighting and sound you'll be using in the show.

721. Be prepared. Don't work on changing your routines during technical rehearsal.

722. At small venues, your prop stand should be so easy to manage that one person can bring it on and off stage.

723. If you wear a wireless microphone, check the battery before the show, and make sure to leave a little slack in the mic cord.

724. Learn, remember and use the crew's names.

725. Change into your costume <u>after</u> you've set up and rehearsed.

726. Don't wear a shirt that shows sweat stains.

727. If your show incorporates improv, look backstage for unusual objects you can incorporate into your act.

728. If you will be using volunteers, check out the audience before the show for likely candidates, but don't get caught peeking out from behind the curtain.

729. Have knowledge of and take advantage of what the venue has to offer you (special lighting effects, knowledgeable staff, etc.).

730. Think of ways to include topical humor that relates to the situation.

731. Be adaptable, and easy to work with.

732. Make sure the technical staff knows and understands your cues.

733. If the client is supposed to pay for your accommodations, verify the arrangements when you check in.

734. Don't over-eat before the show. You don't want to feel heavy and bloated or split your pants during a performance.

735. Be prepared to wait. A lot of shows (especially corporate functions) start much later than originally planned.

736. Just because you're nervous, doesn't mean you have to <u>act</u> like you're nervous. Maintain a relaxed and calm manner backstage.

737. If your hands tend to get sweaty, run them under cold water for a minute and dry them off well before the show to seal the pores.

738. Don't set your props on the floor. Get a prop stand.

739. Never expect to be able to find items you need for your show at the gig unless you specifically ask for them.

740. Make sure any music you use is professionally recorded and edited.

741. If any of your props are breakable, bring a spare.

742. Give each of your props a specific place on your prop stand.

743. Double-check your prop stand before you go on stage to make sure you haven't forgotten anything.

744. Try to watch any performers or speakers who are on before you. Be aware of anything that you might be able to use as a callback.

745. Bring a variety of adapters for any electrical equipment you might be using.

746. Make sure any lit (LED) props are properly charged and you have spares if needed.

747. Have a back-up copy of your music and cue sheets on your phone and stored in the cloud (Drop Box, Google drive or a public folder).

748. Make sure your music is all recorded at the same level.

749. Keep your props in clean and good condition.

750. If you are going to wear a vest, get one that is long enough so that your shirt does not stick out from underneath it.

751. Bring an air pump and spare needle if you are going to be using any type of inflatable ball.

752. Never assume there will be adequate sound and lighting. Get used to performing in many different situations.

753. Make sure your act won't have to compete with food service, people eating, or other noisy distracting activities.

754. Be careful not to do anything that will leave your arms weak or sore too close to show time.

755. Without the proper precautions even a good act can come off looking bad.

756. When shooting a promotional video, it never hurts to pack the audience with friends.

757. When the situation warrants it, (i.e. bright stage lighting) wear make-up.

758. If any of your props have black handles, they may be difficult to see and catch under stage lights. Add a couple of strips of white tape.

759. To keep your props looking good, have two sets. One for practice and one for the stage.

760. If you are using the same props for both the stage and the street, maybe they are not really right for either one.

761. Replace your costume before it starts to look old and worn.

762. Check to see if your fly is zipped up, your teeth are clean, and nothing is hanging out of your nose.

763. Network with other performers whenever you can.

764. The color of your props should not blend in with the color of your costume or the background.

765. Check the stage floor. If it is slippery, you might want to wear rubber soled shoes for better traction.

766. Wear underwear that is the same color as your costume pants, in case you get a rip or zipper malfunction.

767. A headlamp is good backstage when you need to see in the dark and keep your hands free. ❖

During the show

768. Have a digital clock easily visible on stage or in your prop case, and stay within specified time limits.

769. If you sweat a lot or use messy props, have a towel handy.

770. If something is obvious to the audience (i.e. you've split your pants), you might as well mention it and try to get some comedy out of the situation.

771. Don't do inside jokes to entertain your friends who might be in the audience.

772. Start with something that is easy for you to do cleanly. An audience will decide whether they like you or not in the first few minutes. If you have a bad start, the rest of the show can be an uphill battle.

773. Never announce there was something you were going to do – but for some reason, can't.

774. For jugglers ... it's better to do a simple routine flawlessly than a difficult one that is droppy. Most audiences don't know a good juggler from a bad juggler, but they know that a bad juggler drops.

775. Be in the moment. Make sure to keep your shows spontaneous and always be on the lookout for ways to make it more entertaining.

776. Making fun of the venue or technical crew during your show is a good way to keep from being invited back.

777. Make sure an audience volunteer leaves the stage and goes back to their seat as a hero.

778. If the client provides names of volunteers for you to use in your show, make sure they will be the appropriate gender and physical type for the stunt you will be performing.

779. Using a volunteer everyone in the audience knows (the President, CEO, Principal, etc.), is a good way to create a relatable, memorable moment for your show.

780. Make sure you have good hygiene on stage and when interacting with the audience members. Carry breath mints especially if you are a smoker.

781. Don't let little mistakes turn into big mistakes.

782. Never rush through your material. Always give the audience time to respond.

783. Try not to bring volunteers on stage if you don't have something significant for them to do.

784. If you pretend that a bad crowd is a good one, sometimes they are fooled into believing it themselves.

785. Store any props or sound equipment you're not using during the show in a safe place.

786. If wearing a wireless microphone, don't forget about possible damage to the mic pack in your pocket when doing tumbling or pratfalls.

787. Smile! It never hurts to look like you enjoy what you are doing.

788. Don't blame the audience if they are not reacting the way you want them to. Look to see how you can do things differently.

789. Don't acknowledge distractions (hecklers, noises offstage, etc.) that the majority of the audience is unaware of.

790. Deliver MORE than you promise.

791. Don't act as a stagehand. At the end of your act, don't carry off your own prop table.

792. Never joke on stage about how bad your show is. People may believe it.

793. Keep your face active and alive while performing. Your expressions tell a story, and help to keep an audience engaged.

794. When doing walk around gigs, look fabulous so you don't have to work as hard.

795. If you are going to do it, do it right.

796. Always strive for "connection" with the audience.

797. Every performance is a dialogue where the audience responds to you with their laughter and applause. ❖

After the show

798. Be courteous to the next performer. Don't leave a mess.

799. Always thank the crew. Make sure to make it personal and use their names.

800. Leave the dressing room cleaner than you found it.

801. Accept compliments graciously whether you thought you did a good show or not.

802. Accept advice or criticism as well as you do compliments. Never argue with someone else that their "opinion" is wrong about your show.

803. Be accessible. It never hurts to mingle after the show.

804. Have promotional material handy.

805. If someone asks for your card, get theirs too.

806. Follow up a good review with a note of appreciation to the writer.

807. Time how long your show was, and get an idea of each routine's individual length.

808. If any new comedy ideas occurred to you during the show, make sure you have a way to record them, so that you can use them again.

809. Send the client a 'thank you' note.

810. Check to make sure you have all your props, costumes, and sound equipment. Now, check again.

811. Judge a new joke on how it compares to the laughs you usually get with your established material, not to an isolated crowd response.

812. If you work with a partner, never argue with them in front of the client. Save that for the car ride home. ❖

Show Business

Dan Holzman's 5 "R's" of show business
Be Ready, be Reliable, be Resourceful, and
be Really, Really good.

813. Get a deposit and specify how and when you want to receive the balance.

814. Ask for a deposit of 50% up front to confirm the date and reserve it for the client.

815. I prefer the balance of the check due at arrival prior to the performance, but will be flexible if other arrangements are made in advance.

816. Before quoting a price, try to get as much complete information about the gig as possible, including, venue, number of guests, and any past performers they might have had.

817. Get a signed contract and a return plane ticket before accepting any international engagements.

818. It pays to advertise and maintain a healthy social media presence.

819. Select the availability of domain names and social media accounts before picking a stage name.

820. It doesn't matter how much someone says they are going to pay you, if you never get paid.

821. Being an entertainer IS a real job.

822. Don't make excuses for your video. If it's not any good, don't send it out.

823. It's hard to get a $ 5,000 job with a $ 50 video.

824. The first few minutes of your video are most important. It doesn't matter how good it ends if no one makes it that far.

825. Find out what the local acts in your area charge, then charge a bit more and be worth it.

826. If you double your price and you lose half of your gigs, so what?

827. Nobody is going to hire you for a high paying job just because you worked their kid's bar mitzvah for free.

828. Remember, you can't have <u>all</u> the jobs.

829. Be courteous. Just because someone calls you for a low paying job doesn't mean they won't offer you something better in the future.

830. Don't turn a job down by explaining why you don't want to do it. Just tell the client you're "already booked and unavailable."

831. Have benefit rates. Offer the client a discount as an option opposed to a free show.

832. If you get every job you ask for, you are probably not asking for enough money.

833. If you have any doubts about entertainment as a profession – try working an office job for a week.

834. As an entertainer it's hard to schedule long-term commitments. You might only have to work a few days per month, but it's not always the <u>same</u> few days per month.

835. Even if you are the client's first choice, they will probably get someone else if you can't be reached in a timely manner.

836. It's never too early to start a mailing list.

837. Learn to write a press release.

838. Learn to use a personal computer.

839. Set deadlines for yourself and others.

840. If you give people a choice between two prices, they will want to pay the <u>lower</u> price.

841. You get what you pay for. Hire professionals.

842. When competing with another performer, try to get the job because you're the better act, not because you work cheaper.

843. Don't put anything on your promotional video that you're not capable of doing. Don't disappoint the client by offering something that you are not going to deliver.

844. Think long-term.

845. If clients call your home regarding business, leave a professional sounding message on your answering machine.

846. When you are doing business, dress like you are doing business.

847. The secret of selling is ask, ask, ask.

848. Usually the more you are paid, the better you are treated.

849. It is never too early to learn how to save and invest your money.

850. Learn from rejection. Try to find out "why" you didn't get the job.

851. Advertising costs money – but publicity is free.

852. If someone asks you how much you charge, remember, you can always come down from a price you quote – but it's hard to go up.

853. If you can't get higher pay, have premiums that you are willing to negotiate for (first class tickets, lodging, etc.).

854. Get professional photographs, including a headshot, in both black and white and color.

855. Develop items that can be sold or used as promotional tools (t-shirts, videos, etc.).

856. When preparing your promotional materials, don't be surprised if they cost more and take longer for you to get than originally estimated.

857. Keep your video, pictures, and resume up to date.

858. Treat your career as a business. ❖

Guinness World Records

859.   There are a lot more Guinness records that are not published in the book. Check their website for a complete list.

860.   Of the two approaches (beating an old record or setting a new one) beating an old record is an easier route to get approval from Guinness.

861.   Not all records can be beaten. Some become closed at a certain point, so check with Guinness to make sure the category is still open.

862.   Even some records that are not closed may be off limits if someone has paid a fee and is scheduled to attempt it.

863.   Like most things, getting in the book is an odds game. The more you try the better your chances.

864.   To see the king of Guinness records, check out Ashrita Furman, who sets records to honor his guru, Sri Chimnoy.

865.   Do not expect a quick response from Guinness. It might take up to a year to get approval to beat a record.

866.   Submitting a record used to be free, but now a $5.00 fee is charged.

867.   At each step of the submission phase you can pay an extra fee to get fast tracked (it costs about $500 to get an immediate response).

868. The fastest way to get a record is to pay for a Guinness representative to witness and document your record attempt.

869. In addition to a fee you will be required to pay for travel and lodging.

870. The advantages of having a representative are immediate approval and the promotional value to the press for your event.

871. There are several record breaker shows licensed by Guinness to use their name, but each is booked by an independent production company, and like any other TV show you need to know the right person to get booked.

872. If you are interested in setting a duration record, it is important to check the rules to see if breaks can be taken (plus how long and how many).

873. After getting approval from Guinness to break a record, you will get a submission kit that will tell you exactly how to document our attempt.

874. In addition to photographs and video, you will need two letters of expert witness testimony to make sure that all the rules have been followed (the witness must be an expert in field of your attempted record).

875. None of that is needed if an official from Guinness is there to validate your attempt.

876. After you set a record, the certificate (suitable for framing) is sent to you for free.

877. Participants in group records can log in to the website to get a certificate, but one is not sent automatically.

878. You can use the Guinness name in your promo, but the logo is a licensed trademark and you will be sent a cease and desist letter if you attempt to use it without paying for its use (this will be part of the agreement you sign when attempting a record).

879. A great photo of your record will help your chances of getting in the book, so get a professional to cover your attempt.

880. There are about 10 record breaker shows around the world and fees for an appearance are in the $2,500 to $5,000 range (of course there are exceptions but it is usually a good gig to get).

881. You receive no payment for beating a record, but the Guinness name is internationally known and a promo that includes multiple Guinness records sounds impressive.

882. Consider saying "record setter" or "record winner" instead of "record holder" since you will no longer be a "holder" if your record is beaten, and your promo will need to be updated.

883. Decisions by Guinness tend to be arbitrary. Some records are found to be too similar to existing records, or are seemingly turned down for no reason.

884. Decisions seem to be final, and I have heard from a few sources that Guinness can also be disorganized, so patience in dealing with them is a must.

885. In 2018 the I.J.A. is teaming up with Guinness to have a representative at its yearly convention.

886. Juggler and writer for"Magic Magazine" Alan Howard is the Guinness representative for juggling records.

887. Be prepared with significant patience or be willing to pay significant money if you want to be a Guinness World record setter.

888. Other sources to submit records include: recordsetter.com (the easiest way right now) or assistworldrecords.com. ❖

Performing on
America's Got Talent

889. Watch past seasons of A.G.T. to see which acts do well and why.

890. This show is host driven, so think of volunteer stunts that would get them involved.

891. Eat a big breakfast and be prepared for a 10-hour day.

892. You will be asked to stay in costume for most of the day, so make sure you can comfortably do that.

893. You are there to be on TV so try to get on camera as much as possible.

894. Make sure you have a good back story, make it personal and compelling.

895. Study how past winners and competitors have used their appearances for self promotion.

896. Be ready to answer commonly asked questions, for example: "What would you do if you won a million dollars?"

897. If possible, use non-copyrighted music. Understand that the show will have to pay to use popular songs.

898. Work through a producer or an inside contact in order to get a scheduled audition. (See appendix). ❖

Travel

899. When traveling, a hat can be a multipurpose item (for example your pockets can be emptied into it for going through security).

900. When checking in to a hotel, always grab a business card with the hotel's name and address (in the native language).

901. Any bottle with a flip top should be securely wrapped in a plastic bag for traveling.

902. Always iron the bottom part of the dress shirt first. That way you can tuck it into your pants if the iron burns or stains it.

903. Rolled clothing wrinkles less then folded clothing.

904. Make sure to have promotional photos on your phone.

905. Condoms can be used for a variety of purposes while on the road (one example is to protect your mic pack from the rain when working outside).

906. Check to see if any of your equipment is flammable (party poppers for example) and will go against the airline rules for luggage.

907. When leaving your hotel room, place a business card in the electricity slot your key goes in to keep the air conditioning on while you are gone.

908. Don't take the taxis from drivers who contact you inside the airport, they will always be more expensive.

909. If you think you will be traveling a lot, order a passport with extra pages when you apply for one (there is a box you can check off on your application).

910. Bar soap can also be used as shaving cream.

911. Be aware of your body language and hand gestures, especially in foreign countries where they can have different meanings.

912. Know in which countries it is appropriate to barter.

913. It doesn't hurt to be friendly. "You catch more flies with honey then you do with vinegar."

914. The person who sits in the middle on a plane should get both arm rests.

915. I prefer an aisle on long flights, and when booking will check for rows with an empty middle and the window already taken.

916. You can usually gate check larger carry on luggage at your departure gate for free.

917. If you carry your props in a guitar case, you can ask to put it in the closet of the plane's galley.

918. Sometimes it is easier to refer to your props when dealing with the airlines as sporting equipment.

919.   Travel with an empty water bottle. Most airports have a place to fill them up with filtered water.

920.   You can use a blow dryer to dry damp clothes, but don't use it for too long or it will burn out.

921.   Roll wet clothes in a towel to wring them out before ironing.

922.   Fold your suit inside out for fewer wrinkles.

923.   Earplugs or noise cancelling headphones can make a noisy plane flight more endurable.

924.   Travel sometimes requires you to learn regional toilet techniques. (For example: "The squatty potty").

925.   Clothes pins can come in handy on the road (one example is to pin window curtains closed).

926.   For international gigs, make sure you know what currency you are being paid in.

927.   You may want to bring your own small sound system even if one will be provided, as it can come in handy if you encounter technical difficulties.

928.   If your suitcase is full of unusual props, consider including a photo of you using them, in your luggage.

929.   Make sure your suitcase is always tagged with your I.D. including your cell phone number and email address.

930.   If you plan to nap on long flights, make sure to tell the cabin attendant to wake you up for meals.

931. Go ahead and ask for a full can of soda when drinks are offered, the airline can afford it.

932. Travel with a Tide detergent stick.

933. Febreze spray can freshen up your dirty clothing and give them a couple extra days of wear when a washing machine is not handy.

934. Make sure to put stickers and other identifying marks on your luggage. You want it to stick out from the crowd and be easily to identify.

935. When traveling to areas that are known to be difficult to always get paid in, try to get 50% up front, 25% on arrival and 25% at the end of the gig.

936. Never travel to a foreign country without a return ticket, and keep track of your passport at all times.

937. Make sure to check when your frequent flyer miles expire. You don't want to waste them.

938. If you forget your frequent flyer number while traveling, you have 6 months to collect them, so save your tickets.

939. A black permanent marker can be great for touch ups for black dress shoes.

940. Check the special meal options. Even if you are not a vegetarian, sometimes that meal is better than the airline mystery meat.

941. If you are going to get stuck in the middle, you might as well get one towards the front of the plane.

942. Keep your suitcases and bags off the hotel room floor and closed when not in use to lessen the chance of getting bed bugs.

943. Hotel glasses are notoriously dirty; only drink from individually wrapped plastic cups.

944. When checking out from your room, move around it in a clockwise fashion to make sure you have not forgotten everything.

945. My favorite term for the one last look to make sure you have all your belongings is "The Idiot-Check" don't be an idiot and leave anything behind.

946. Make sure to know the exact number of bags you are travelling with at all times, and do a visual count of them before departing any location.

947. When traveling with your equipment in your car,- make sure you are able to see it out of the window while you are eating at a restaurant. Park where there is plenty of light and a security camera when possible.

948. When going through the airport x-ray machine put your shoes and belt in first. That way you can put them on while waiting for the rest of your bags.

949. Be aware that you can ask for a late check out from your hotel room at no extra charge. It will only be a few hours, but you might as well take advantage of the extra time if needed.

950. When using a public bathroom, always check to make sure there is enough toilet paper before committing to a stall.

951. Travel with a small door stop to keep your room secure while you are sleeping.

952. If your suitcase has a combination lock make sure to change it after opening so no one who cleans the room can make a note of the combination for a later time.

953. If you desire a firmer mattress, sleep on the opposite side of where the alarm clock is. Most people choose that side and the mattress will be softer there.

954. Even if you don't use them, check all the hotel room drawers to see if anything useful has been left behind.

955. Bring a towel while flying. It can be used as a blanket, pillow, neck rest, and if something spills you'll have it handy to clean it up right away.

956. Leave your wallet with hotel door-key inside next to your night-stand. In an emergency (for example, a fire alarm at night), you can grab your wallet on the way out the door.

957. Put a business card INSIDE each bag in the event the luggage tag tears off while being tossed around by baggage handlers.

958. Pack two days of needed medication on your person in the event your luggage is lost.

959. If you are hit by a case of diarrhea, try Imodium for fast relief.

960. If you're a repeat guest at a hotel, make note of staff who were helpful. Positive feedback is important to their continued livelihood.

961. Travel with an eye mask and earplugs for undisturbed sleep.

962. When international travel coming up, slowly shift in advance to the new time zone so you can arrive pre-adjusted.

963. When leaving your empty hotel room, turn around and loudly say "yeah I'll be back soon," so any potential thieves lurking nearby will think there's someone else in the room.

964. Replace as much physical luggage as you can with apps. (maps, guidebooks, etc.).

965. Pack a flashlight (get silver or yellow, never a black one since they are hard to see in the dark).

966. Travel-sized Handi-Wipes can really be handy when a washroom is not easily accessible.

967. Put your clothes immediately in the washer when you return home to kill off any bugs picked up on the road.

968. When flying , split your props in half so you can do a show if only one piece of luggage arrives.

969. The most forgotten thing is charger cords. The front desk of any hotel chain will often have replacements if you left yours behind.

970. Always check to see if the alarm has been set by the guest before you. There is nothing like an unplanned 5:30 am wake up buzzer to start your day off on a bad note.

971. Bring your own small travel alarm clock that you can trust.

972. Have disinfectant wipes to wipe down various gross items in the room, phone, remote, door handles, faucet, tv buttons, and anything people mindlessly touch.

973. Pack up and organize as much as possible the night before you check out, and after dressing, double check everything in the room, top to bottom.

974. Use some form of Aroma-Therapy in the room to cleanse old energies, and make your stay more comfortable.

975. Call housekeeping to advise them that you won't require service. For security the fewer people going into your room the better.

976. You can cook food on your defroster setting while driving long distances. Give 2 hours on high for something that takes an hour in the oven.

977. Silicone ear plugs work way better than foam ones.

978.   Body weight exercises require very little space. You can easily train every muscle group in your room. Consider also bringing a jump rope. Traveling is no excuse to ignore your physical health.

979.   Bring some nutritious snacks to cover your entire trip, just in case you can't find healthy options along the way.

980.   Bring your own pillow case. Many hotels use a harsh detergent that can irritate sensitive skin.

981.   Always steal the pen and note book that is in every hotel room, and take all the offered toiletries. If you don't want them, consider giving them away to the homeless.

982.   If you call in advance and tell the front desk that you are traveling with temperature sensitive medications they will usually make sure a small fridge is in the hotel room waiting for you.

983.   Put bright fluorescent stickers on your phone chargers, that way you never forget them by leaving them in the sockets as you leave the hotel room.

984.   Bring electrical adapters needed for US products to plug into when traveling to international destinations.

985.   Wheels on your cases can add ease of transport, but also add up to 8 lbs per bag.

986.   Use a hair dryer to heat up leftover pizza.

987. Always use a sanitizer to wipe down the TV remote control. It is known to be the dirtiest, germ ridden item in the room.

988. Don't trust the safe in the room. It can be easy to open them for thieves who know how. If you are going to use it, make sure it is secured to the wall.

989. If there is a free breakfast buffet at your hotel, use the tray under the coffee maker to bring breakfast back to your room.

990. To cancel a hotel reservation after the refund deadline, call and say the date needs to be changed to the following week, then you can phone back a couple days later and cancel without them charging you.

991. Grab a couple of the hotel business cards and carry them with you. If you get lost, you can always hand one to a cab driver to show them where to go.

992. Before checking out, straighten the bedspread to make sure nothing was laid on the bed and is still being covered.

993. If you travel a ton, take a picture of your room number so you don't go to the room you were in the night before at a different hotel.

994. Hotel shower caps make great shoe covers when packing.

995. When traveling have at least 2 different brands of credit cards. That way, if one is denied you'll have a spare.

996. As you undress, put your billfold, keys, cell phone, and other pocket items in one of your shoes. That way, you won't leave them behind as you dress the next morning.

997. Take a picture of the parking spot number your car is parked on in case you forget.

998. When renting a car, always ask for their "corporate rate" or CAA discount at the desk. It saves about $10 to $50 every time.

999. When you need ice for beer, forget the tiny ice bucket. Take your room's empty trash can to the ice machine. It's much bigger.

1,000. A good way to get stuff done for you in a hotel is to get a hotel employee name to use in your request.

1,001. Always remember to bring along a good book to read. ❖

Be Funnier

WITH SCOTTY MELTZER
AND DAN HOLZMAN:

WORKING THE FOUR STEPS OF DAN
HOLZMAN'S FRAMEWORK TECHNIQUE

DAN'S FOUR STEPS

• STEP ONE: CHOOSE A TRICK

You start by choosing a trick, stunt, or skill to build your routine around. Dan calls this "the framework stunt" because it will form the framework of your routine.

For Dan's Framework Technique, you're looking for a trick that has enough inherent interest to stand on its own, even before you have any good material for it. It should something you can do consistently without dropping and that has a natural beginning, middle, and end.

It's even better if the trick is funny by itself, and of course it's much better if the trick is original! Why spend your time writing funny, original jokes around a trick that other jugglers perform when you can spend the same amount of time creating a routine that's unique in all its aspects?

Some ways to approach creating an original trick might be:

Learn a skill no one else is performing.

Combine two or more skills that you haven't seen put together before.

Find a unique prop to manipulate.

Choose a subject no one else is talking about and ask: "How can I illustrate this using my particular skills."

Ask yourself: "How can I express an old idea in a new way, a new idea in an old way, or best of all a new idea in new way?"

Think about stunts you've never seen but would want to.

Research older stunts and tricks to uncover one that no one is currently doing.

Start with a common skill and ask: "How can I do this differently?"

Look at non-juggling performance art forms and ask: "What could I add to this to make it my own?"

The inspiration for this framework stunt in Dan's show came from a written description of a trick performed by 19th century juggler Paul Cinquevalli:

Cinquevalli would juggle a knife, turnip, and fork in one hand while holding a blowgun in the other. He then blew a dart into the turnip, threw the fork into it and caught both together on the knife.

Dan started with this because he believed it would be a strong, compelling trick with a clear beginning, middle, and end that no other performer was currently doing.

- **STEP TWO: ADD THE VITAL INFORMATION THE AUDIENCE NEEDS TO FOLLOW THE TRICK**

During this step you're creating the bones of the routine without trying to be funny. You're just making sure the audience isn't confused and getting them interested in what's about to happen.

Here's what Dan's script was like at this step with just the vital information:

"I am going to juggle a fork and an apple with my right hand and hold a blowgun to my mouth with my left hand. I will throw the apple high into the air, shoot it with a blow dart, and then catch it on the tip of the fork."

(Notice how Dan cleverly simplified the trick to make sure it was something he could do successfully every time.)

At this point, you should have a simple routine that you could perform. It may not be funny yet, but it should be effective and entertaining even in this basic form.

So do it. Go out and try this bare bones routine onstage and see what happens.

When Dan first performed his bare bones version, he discovered that a standard blowgun dart was too small for the audience to see, so he changed the props from an apple, a tiny dart, and a fork to a cabbage, a bigger custom-made dart, and a battle-axe.

What happened when you performed yours?

Did you drop too much? Then make the trick easier. Simplify it. You can always make it harder later when you're more comfortable with the base stunt.

Did the audience laugh at anything? Keep that! Did they yell anything funny at you? Add that!

Can you think of ways to add more inherent interest or comedy potential to the base stunt? If you can, try 'em. Make your base stronger.

Does the audience understand what's happening? Nope? Then work more on Step Two.

Did they care? No? Go back to Step One.

They dug it? Great! It's time to move on to Step Three.

• STEP THREE: EMBELLISH THE NARRATIVE

Here's where you put some meat on those bones. You're embellishing not just to make the trick more theatrical, but also to generate setups to write jokes from. You're adding information because, as Dan likes to say, "There's no comedy without information."

Start with the truth. Add in a lie. Bring in more information.

Ask yourself: Where did I learn this? How long have I done this? Why did I learn this? What could go right? What will go wrong? (Mike Goudeau thinks the last three of these are the most important comic questions to ask yourself.)

You can improvise around that basic narrative, and bring in information that isn't already in the story.

You can experiment with different emotions, expressions, gestures, character choices, premises, and choreography.

These embellishments can accomplish two important things:

Add to the interest that should already be inherent in the stunt, and

Create more comic potential for you to exploit in Step Four.

Here's a sample of some embellished dialogue:

"Ladies and gentlemen, you are about to see a

stunt that hasn't even been attempted for over 100 years, since it was last performed by that great juggler: the late Paul Cinquevalli. This trick requires me to use three different, dangerous props, a very real battle-axe, an authentic jungle blowgun, and a leafy green head of cabbage."

• STEP FOUR: WRITE JOKES BASED ON THAT EMBELLISHED NARRATIVE

When writing jokes based on your embellished narrative, you can build on any comic elements or joke formats you want, using all the different joke writing methods you know.

And remember, when we write jokes, we aren't limiting ourselves to verbal jokes with formal setups and punchlines. We're also looking for physical gags, takes, comic reactions, audience interactions, and anything else that we find funny.

It's great to be able to sit down, write a bunch of jokes, and then later choose the good ones. It's a skill and discipline we should all have.

But writing jokes doesn't have to mean sitting at a desk, staring at an empty Word doc. You can also write jokes by ad-libbing onstage, rehearsing with intent, modeling our comic heroes, and jamming with our friends.

I call anything that gets a laugh a "joke" and any way you can find those laughs "writing jokes."

Your embellishments can become setups for all kinds of jokes:

Any flowery embellishments you added in Step Three are perfect launching points for exaggeration jokes. Analogies can lead you to mixes. A visual image can become a visual metaphor joke. Statements are great setups for reverse jokes.

Want more comic potential? Write association lists and assumption lists based on your embellishments and the true facts of the vital information.

Mine those lists and your embellished dialogue for comic connectors. Look for words with multiple meanings and ambiguities within your story. Can't find any? Add ambiguity by turning nouns into pronouns or turning gendered pronouns into neutral ones.

Look for clichés to exploit with reference, reverse, and mix jokes.

Are you leading your audience to expect something? Try leading them away instead.

What props are you using? Write association lists and assumption lists for each and discover the laughs hiding within.

How can you tag your new jokes? What can you act out? What can you call back to?

Here are three jokes Dan wrote for this article, inspired by the sample embellished dialogue above:

"You are about to see a stunt that was performed by the late juggler Paul Cinquevalli. He's not dead. He just never shows up on time."

"This very dangerous trick was last performed by the great juggler Paul Cinquevalli over 150 years ago, and now he's dead. Coincidence? I don't think so."

"This trick requires me to use a real … looking battle-axe, an authentic jungle blow gun I bought on eBay, and from Whole Foods Market this $55 cabbage."

WORKING THE STEPS

One nice feature of Dan Holzman's Four-Step Framework Technique is that it leads you through the process of creating a performance-ready routine.

By the end of Step Two you've got a stripped down, bare-bones routine that you can easily slip into the middle of your show.

After Step Three you'll have an even longer routine with lots of new setups that, like my juggling partner, are just begging for punches.

And by the time you've completed Step Four you'll have a strong routine, with compelling dialogue and a bunch of new jokes ready to try in front of your next audience.

AN EXAMPLE

As an exercise to go with this article, Dan and I decided to put his Framework Technique to the test and write a new routine together, starting with nothing but his Four-Step Technique and our mutual respect and disdain for each other.

Here's what we came up with:

STEP ONE: CHOOSE A TRICK

We started with a commonly done gag: The Ping Pong Ball Balance (using rubber cement to fake-balance a ping pong ball on your nose). We asked ourselves, "How can we do this differently? What else could we fake-balance? What could we combine with this?"

We thought about cigarettes and straws, a pen or a match, dollar bills, poker chips, playing cards …

Playing cards? A magic trick where the selected card ends up balanced on Dan's nose?

That seems good enough for a framework stunt.

STEP TWO: ADD THE VITAL INFORMATION THE AUDIENCE NEEDS TO FOLLOW THE TRICK

"Sir, pick a card any card. Sign it. Place it back into the deck. I'm going to find your card using only my face. (Dan rubs the cards all over his face, ending up with one card balanced or stuck on his nose.) Is this your card?"

That seems good enough to try onstage.

Time to buy some rubber cement, learn how to hold a break, palm a card, and do a street show.

STEP THREE: EMBELLISH THE NARRATIVE

"I have here a deck of ordinary playing cards. All 52 are different. I'm going to do something with these cards that no other magician would even attempt. I need the help of someone from the audience who is not easily influenced. You sir. Are you easily influenced? No. Great. Pick a card. Any card. You had a completely free choice?

Good. Now sign that card. Place it back into the deck. Some magicians use sleight of hand. I'm going to use sleight of face. I'm going to find your card using only my incredibly handsome, rugged, and masculine face. (Dan rubs the cards all over his face, ending up with the card fake-balanced on his nose.) Sir, is this your card?"

STEP FOUR: WRITE JOKES BASED ON THAT EMBELLISHED NARRATIVE

1)   (Before starting the card trick part of this routine, have your volunteer sign a $20 bill. Take it. Vanish it.) Okay we'll do something more fun: A card trick. Pick a card. Any card. You have a completely free choice. Well, not completely free. It's already cost you 20 bucks.

2)   You have a completely free choice, unlike in this election.

3)   We start with a completely free choice of a forced playing card.

4)   I need someone to pick a card. I need someone who is not easily influenced or swayed. Not a Trump voter.

5)   I need a volunteer who's an independent thinker. Someone who's not easily influenced by a stranger. You sir, would you put your hand up for me? (If he raises his hand) Okay then, not you.

6)   You sir. Can you confirm that you are not a paid stooge. Just a hobby then?

7)   You pick the card. And you, (to a child) you get to

choose the part of my face I'm going to use to find that card. My nose? You've picked my nose? In front of all these people you're going to pick my nose? Ewww ... Gross!

8) **SCOTTY:** If my face was on a playing card, it would be the King of Hearts.

   TRINK: Yeah, 'cause that's the one with a knife through its head.

9) **SCOTTY:** A great magician can find your card using only his rugged, manly, handsome face.

   TRINK: Unfortunately THIS is the only one he has.

10) I'm going to find your signed card with my nose. First I must get your scent. (Sniff the volunteer like a dog would.) Now the cards. (Sniff and search the cards. Rub one card a lot with your nose. Choose the wrong card and ask ...) Is this your card.? No? It's not.? You're right. It's snot. (Showing the snotty card) Get it? It's SNOT! (Reacting to the expected groan) That joke used to kill when I was five. I don't know what happened. I must be delivering it wrong. But watch this ... (throw the deck in the air. As your hand comes down from throwing the deck, palm the card onto your nose where it will stick on the rubber cement you prepped before the trick.) How about this one? Is this your card? (It is!)

OUR RESULTS

Dan and I worked together for about 15 minutes coming up with this, and then I put in another couple of hours by myself organizing and typing it up, adding a couple of additional jokes along the way.

We bet if you put in the time, you can come up with something even better!

(Long pause.)

It's now been three months since Dan and I wrote that routine, and I still haven't gone onstage to try the whole thing. I guess my final advice to you is, "Do as I say, not as I don't do."

I did, at least, get around to trying some of the jokes. Here are my results:

#1 is too close to an Amazing Jonathon joke for me, so that's out.

I don't like #2, because it brings in the election without taking a position. I skipped it.

I tried #3. It didn't get a laugh. Too bad. I liked that one.

Prior to the election, #4 got more of a cheer than a laugh in one show and a mixed cheer/boo in another. Now that the election is over, so is the window for that short-lived topical joke.

#5 worked well enough for me to keep in the show … for now.

#6 didn't work at all, which really surprised me. I thought that one would be a keeper. Katrine thinks it died because the word "stooge" is out-of-date, like doing a joke about an LP where the connector is "groovy."

I haven't tried #7, #8, or #9 yet.

The "snot" beat in #10 is too close to a Penn & Teller joke, so I cut that, but sniffing the volunteer to get his scent worked quite well. I'm going to keep that in the show and play with some tags for it.

So I got one new joke that will work with any volunteer bit in my show and a completely new routine to work on when I get around to it, and Dan and I haven't spoken in three months.

I call that a win-win.

HOMEWORK

Pick a trick. Write a narrative. Embellish it. Write some jokes.

Appendix

Page 4   http://legacy.worldclown.com

Page 12.   www.threefingerjuggling.com

Page 32.   soapbubblewikia.com

Page 36.   www.adamwinrichwhips.com

Page 46.   www.broadbentboomerangs.com

Page 48.   www.westernstageprops.com

Page 54   www. Realstraightjackets.com
                www. Monkeydungeon.com.

Page 64.   churchstmarketplace@gmail.com
                scottm@comedyindustries.com.

Page 78.   www.buskercentral.com

Page 79.   www.bramson.com
                www.dcptalent.com
                www.spolightentertainment.com

Page 110.   recordsetter.com
                assistworldrecords.com

Page 111.   joegunches@gmail.com (put AGT in the
                subject line).

Travel   Rolling Cart
                Utility Wagon
                Tri-Kart 800
                www.kart-a-bag.com

About the Author

Daniel Holzman worked as one-half of the highly successful juggling team The Raspyni Brothers for 35 years. He and his partner Barry Friedman appeared on the *Tonight Show* with Johnny Carson, performed for President Reagan at Ford's Theatre and won two I.J.A. team competitions. Daniel Holzman is also an active solo performer, podcaster, has set two Guinness Book world records, and is the inventor of a brand new skill toy "The Ringdama."

Made in the USA
Middletown, DE
11 August 2023